THE INVENTION
OF LIBERTY

THE INVENTION
OF LIBERTY

1700-1789

JEAN STAROBINSKI

SKIRA

RIZZOLI
NEW YORK

First published 1964
First paperback edition 1987

Published in the United States of America in 1987 by

Rizzoli INTERNATIONAL PUBLICATIONS, INC.
597 Fifth Avenue/New York 10017

© 1987 by Editions d'Art Albert Skira S.A., Geneva

Translated from the French by Bernard C. Swift

Printed in Switzerland

Library of Congress Cataloging-in-Publication Data
Starobinski, Jean.
   The invention of liberty, 1700-1789.

   Translation of: L'invention de la liberté, 1700-1789.
   Bibliography: p.
   Includes index.
   1. Art, Modern—17th-18th centuries—Europe—Themes,
motives.   2. Aesthetics.   3. Eighteenth century.
I. Title.
N6756.S7313   1987   709'.03'3   87-9851
ISBN 0-8478-0846-7 (pbk.)

I

MAN'S UNIVERSE
IN THE 18TH CENTURY

ACTION AND SENSATION

The eighteenth century must be distinguished from its legend. In the early nineteenth century, Europe began to conjure up a nostalgic picture of the preceding century as an age of elegance and frivolity, of sharp wit and uninhibited manners, solely intent on the culpable and delightful pursuit of unrestrained enjoyment. The century of iron, of industry, of democratic revolutions saw another age fading into the past, complete with its masks and gay ribbons, a golden age of mellow, comfortable living, in which even death and war, with their flourish of fine lace, were supposedly neither real death nor real war. Especially after the mid-century the nostalgia and desire for self-justification of the well-to-do led them to construct a philosophy of history—consisting of a mythology of the *ancien régime*. This philosophy combined a longing for the eighteenth century's unrestricted gaiety with an indictment of its fatal irresponsibility. For though the bourgeois classes would have liked to retain certain aspects of this vanished age, they were forced to admit that like an attractive fruit hiding and nourishing a worm the eighteenth century contained a sense of nihilism which was to facilitate the development of the "subversive spirit." The middle classes owed everything to the Revolution, yet they regarded the Revolution as the breach through which evil had entered the world. The parks of Watteau, the boudoirs of Boucher, the carnivals of Guardi all seemed to be the images of a paradise already tormented by melancholy at the prospect of its own destruction, mortally wounded by a *fault* implicit in its pleasures. The official thinkers of respectable society in the nineteenth century deplored the moral corruption of the preceding century; but this same society preferred "Louis XV" furniture, collected libertine prints, and for its amusements dressed up in swords, silk breeches, powdered wigs and black velvet masks... The range of eighteenth-century properties induced an atmosphere of light-hearted love-making, of spicy seduction, of amorous, perfumed conquests. Of course these bourgeois

fancy-dress balls were merely imitations; but sanctioned by an "artistic" cult of the past they provided an excuse to evade the repressive rules of a strait-laced "Victorian" morality for the space of an evening. Where the nostalgia of the "humanist" age, from the fifteenth to the eighteenth century, with its classical education, had sought its aesthetic alibi in the pagan myths, the nineteenth century, no longer familiar with Ovid, had recourse to a falsified image of a "frivolous" eighteenth century: a make-believe world in which they could savor theoretically, and therefore inoffensively, the delights of a bygone freedom and licentiousness. Even serious historians tended to evoke an eighteenth century as unlike the reality of that century as the Alexanders and Venuses of the Rococo opera were unlike the gods and heroes of antiquity.

We must try to show the eighteenth century as it really was, in all its complexity and gravity, with its taste for the original reassessments of great principles; for it is still present behind all our contemporary undertakings and problems. We are historians: it produced or at least imposed the modern notion of history. We contemplate the arts: it saw the rise of independent aesthetic reflection. If in the actual practice of the fine arts it was not a century of decisive revolution it was at least open to experimentation, exaggerations and conflicts. Critics and philosophers began to voice their opinions about the arts (sometimes untowardly). For they did not merely argue about the *means* chosen by the artist, they examined its *ends* and the possibility of making enlightened *judgments* which might reveal the essential characteristics of the beautiful and the sublime. The men of the eighteenth century were not content simply to experience the pleasure afforded by works of art: they wanted to assess the particular characteristics of these works and situate them in the perspective of some universal plan of the development of humanity. These anxious critical questions about the function of art did eventually have some effect on the artists themselves, though the aesthetic theories did not necessarily influence them immediately; but Diderot's *Salons* and his *Essai sur la Peinture*, Burke's *Enquiry*, Lessing's *Laocoon* not only commented on works of art already completed, they evoked a still unrealized art and outlined a potential creative mind which the next generation of artists were to emulate in their works and in their lives.

Diderot had already observed that the language of the theorist is often so vague that the most dissimilar works of art can be embraced by a single statement of abstract principles. "How frequently and easily two persons using exactly the same expressions may be thinking and actually saying two quite different things." During the century of Enlightenment everyone invoked nature, but each understood nature after his own fashion. Nature according to Hogarth is not nature as Chardin sees it. The history of the aesthetic theories of the eighteenth century would not in itself help us to define the art of the century, for the theorists were blind to many aspects of the art, and the artists for their part were unable to fulfill many of the theoretical requirements. Philosophers (Bosanquet, Cassirer, etc.) and art historians studied respectively—quite independently and each according to his own predilections—the evolution of ideas or artistic creation. This was no doubt a legitimate division of their interests but it is unsatisfactory if we wish to grasp the living reality of the eighteenth century. We must avoid interpreting the art or the thought in isolation from each other—they are largely indivisible, with a common historical and social origin; our task is to unravel and synthesize the complex interrelation of an art moving towards liberation and the highly demanding reflection which was trying to understand this art, to guide and inspire it.

This is a far cry from the image of a frivolous eighteenth century. At the same time, however, the picture of licentiousness to which it has tended to be reduced is not altogether unjustified. It represents one of many experiments possible with liberty: libertinism is an aspect of precisely that liberty without which little progress would have been possible in philosophical reflection. The most representative men of the century desired their freedom in order to seek alike immediate pleasure and fundamental truths; they sought enjoyment, but also critical understanding.

According to many observers, dissipation was considered a necessary palliative to extreme boredom and despondency: by giving the senses full rein it was supposed possible to gain a clearer awareness of actually being alive. The same held for complete freedom in abstract speculation: the mere act of thinking, however confusedly, involves an implicit "I exist" which could be endangered if speculation were abandoned. To opt for abstract reflection as opposed to sensual libertinism is simply to free oneself to some extent from external objects and seek happiness in the handling of ideas rather than in the immediate sensory pleasures of life.

At the beginning of the century the philosopher John Locke formulated, in theory, this attitude towards life. Opposing Descartes, who maintained that the "soul" thinks continuously, possesses innate ideas and is therefore always assured of its own existence, Locke affirmed that the soul has ideas only *after* sensations and that thought depends entirely on material supplied by sensory experience: far from being able to depend on innate ideas the soul is only conscious of its existence at the instant of sensation, or when reflection actively compares the traces left by sensations. So nothing is more variable than our consciousness of existing, and nothing is more necessary than to try to vary our sensations and thereby to multiply our ideas. An unoccupied mind is in a sense annihilated. Fortunately, natural human impatience and uneasiness never leave us in peace: we are forever urged to escape from the anxiety of emptiness and to seek, through outside sensations and fleeting thoughts, a fullness and intensity that must be continually renewed. This particular style of living characterizes the *aimlessness* of the eighteenth century: all its activities are fugitive and ephemeral, from the pursuit of pleasure to the expansion of trading or the exploration of nature, for they belong entirely to the present moment, and that moment is instantly past. Yet beyond what has been attained, and thereby lost, our uneasiness perceives a new requirement in which life may find confirmation and renewal. To avoid absolute dejection men need to provide themselves with passions: this is the lesson running through a book which was to exert a lasting influence on the aesthetics of the eighteenth century, the *Réflexions critiques sur la poésie et la peinture* by the Abbé Du Bos (1718): "The soul, like the body, has its particular needs. One of man's greatest needs is to have his mind occupied. Boredom follows close on inaction of the mind and to avoid the torments of this painful evil men often undertake the most demanding tasks... The excitement caused by our passions, even in solitude, is indeed so keen that any other state is by comparison nothing more than dull inertia. So we instinctively seek out objects capable of exciting our passions, even though these objects may give rise to confusion of mind, restless nights and days of anguish: but as a general rule men suffer more from the *absence* of passions than from the anxieties caused by these passions."

From the outset, the theoretical reasoning of this "rationalist" century recognized the absolute domination of passion in poetry and the fine arts. It is true that the images of the passions evoked in 1718 are not so vehement as those of the Romantics, but from the very beginning the work of art was given the psychological function of exciting the emotions through surprise and intensity. The work could be defined in terms of its subjective effect: it was to jolt the mind out of sluggishness and idleness, and by means of vivid images evoke an instant of high emotion and excitement, of mental or physical stimulation. Following the tradition of profane humanism, art was directed towards the individual—amateur or specialist. With the invention of perspective, as Panofsky has shown, a picture is presented to an individual consciousness which is in the privileged position of controlling the "point of view" around which the pictorial space is organized. If, as a result, this isolated human consciousness comes to experience its own "duration" as a succession of intermittent instants, divided by long periods of negation, this will not deprive it of its central, privileged position; in the event, however, we find that aesthetic emotion was merely one of

the resources which men used excessively in order to intensify and stimulate the momentary joy of sensing their own vital existence. Consequently art itself was to become more expressive, impetuous, delicate; by an ever more vivid representation of anguish, pleasure or uncertainty art could the better induce these emotions in the observer. Images were therefore to be used for their inherent "eloquence," for the moral value of their narrative content; pictures were to represent a moment of pathos, or a witty, piquant scene, so that the observer's sympathetic reaction might produce in him an analogous emotion, a compassionate or a terrified response. A fleeting moment of time, caught and immobilized in the painting, was to combine immediate impact with discursive statement.

Paintings of historical scenes, for example, tried to overcome the disadvantages of their temporal immobility by capturing the essence of an event in its movement from a still perceptible past into an imminent future. This was an "impure" use of the image, typical of many eighteenth-century illustrations and anecdotic prints.

But the "enlightened" man who constantly claimed the right to contradict all previously accepted authorities acquired thereby a sense of oppositions which enabled him also to contradict himself. For all its temptations and cherished formulas, the eighteenth century fostered a lively spirit of criticism and sometimes a resolute and viable autocriticism, with a desire to experiment with opposites. Thus, during the Neoclassical period, a taste for depicting *eternal* beauty was to replace the immediate fleeting enjoyments of the Rococo: mobility of expression wished to be forgotten in immobility of form.

FREEDOM: THE POLITICAL AND ARTISTIC CONTEXT

From the time of the *fêtes galantes* to the appearance on the Revolutionary battlefields of the tricolor with its motto of "Liberty or Death," the history of the eighteenth century could be regarded as a stage on which an aspiration towards liberty crystallizes, bursts and shatters in the clash of arms. Not that this sequence actually led to the reign of liberty, but throughout the century the idea of liberty was tried out, both in the form of an abusive capriciousness and of a protestation *against* abuses. The taste for living freely sometimes consisted of an unbridled search for pleasure, sometimes of a demand for the renewal of moral standards, and some writers (such as Fielding or Restif de la Bretonne) combined the two tendencies confusedly. These demands for freedom were stimulated, clarified and strengthened in proportion to the energy and power of those who sought to oppose it. The need for liberty thrives on opposition. The history of the eighteenth century records the struggle—occasionally the dialogue—between the demands of autocratic powers and the reactions of men who refused to submit. In politics, as in morals and religion, the established relationship between sovereign authority and obedient subjects no longer seemed justifiable. As Kant was to say, the men of the Enlightenment were no longer willing to obey arbitrary external laws; they wanted personal autonomy to recognize only such laws as they perceived within themselves.

The development of industries and vast urban growth created new forms of servitude and new political and economic problems; had the restriction of liberty not been so widespread, the demand for liberty would not have been so insistent. The insolence of the rich, the blundering of those in power, oppression from above, all contributed to the realization that a minority was using its extreme liberty to destroy the liberty of the rest. From Louis XIV's final wars to the holocaust of Napoleon, the history of the century reads like the blood-soaked maturing of the concept of the Nation.

The philosophers would certainly have liked to alter this course of history. Their desire for freedom and their impatience with obstructions prompted them to set down on paper the speculative image of the liberty they demanded, in terms of what was actually possible. "Man is born free," said Rousseau; and the individual was not to be deprived of his natural freedom on entering society and becoming a citizen. But "everywhere he is in chains": the problem was to find a social system in which the necessity of social order and individual freedom might not be contradictory. Rousseau and his contemporaries were well aware of the difficulty of these problems; they considered that a solution should be possible by means of a new "social art." The term is emblematic: it characterizes an age in which the word "art" had not yet been narrowed, specialized, purified. An art is any method which tends to improve and perfect a natural phenomenon, to make it more orderly, agreeable and useful. By a perfect transmutation of natural liberty into civil liberty, and by reconciling the security of the individual and the authority of the State, the legislator would be exercising supreme art. The enlightened reasoning of Locke, of Montesquieu, was already prepared to apportion rationally the influence of the prince (which tends spontaneously towards tyranny) and the natural desires of the individual (which inevitably conflict and lead to anarchy). Self-interest might, of course, have restrained both princes and peoples; they could have found sensible means of compromise and inspired respect for the law. But reason often goes unheeded and one's own self-interest is often elusive. Neither the despots, the highly successful middle-classes, nor the populace exasperated by abuses were aware of their own true interests. From the European mainland, England seemed to assure the liberty of its citizens by a wise system of separating the powers. But in the second half of the century this envied ideal was no longer so clear-cut; a new, federal ideal was arising beyond the Atlantic, where the American settlers were establishing their community in tolerance and moderation. It seemed that the supreme social art was going to be achieved amongst men who knew relatively little about European culture, with its luxury and social fragmentation.

In the history of the eighteenth century the fine arts do not simply comprise an indirect source of information, a series of supporting documents: they are part and parcel of the adventure. The status of art and the artist underwent a change which, though not immediately evident in visible artistic *form*, was in the long run none the less decisive. Through the claims of the artists and the experiments of aesthetic philosophy (a further invention of the century) a particular idea of artistic creation evolved: the work of art came to be considered as the highest manifestation of man's fully autonomous consciousness. Poets, musicians, painters—gripped by a new spirit and urged on by a new public—became the privileged trustees and sometimes the prophets of a spirit of freedom otherwise universally jeopardized. In a sense this transference of responsibility to the artist indicates the limitations of the basic liberty which the practical politicians fought for: a higher liberty existed on the plane of the imagination and interiority.

It has often been insufficiently stressed that art, at any historical period whatsoever, is not a direct expression of the universal state of a given society: it is primarily the prerogative of the wealthy and the powerful, who order works of art and appreciate them according to the criteria of their own tastes and culture. Art should be evaluated partly in function of the sociological circumstances of its creation, certain social groups being perhaps excluded from both creation and contemplation. What is the relationship between the work of art and the silent world which has no access to the diverse languages of culture? Nor should it be forgotten that the patron who acquires a painting, a statue, a building, may himself determine what function the work shall

have. He may retain it for his private enjoyment; or conversely, he may invite the general public to come and admire marvels in which the genius of the artist sometimes counts less than his own prestige in having made the creation materially possible. Where persons from lower social classes seem to be excluded from the producer-consumer circuit of "beauty," they may still be included amongst the recipients who are to be assembled together, edified and amazed. In opposition to the private collection of the amateur, built up for his own undivided pleasure, there are churches and public squares which are offered openly to the people so that they may recognize in them the symbols of their faith, the *space* of their communal life: they may collectively appropriate and identify themselves with such works. To analyze the function of art it is essential to ask not only who is speaking and why, but also who is being addressed and whether the intended recipient has actually understood the work.

If he has sufficient leisure a painter can create for the pleasure of creating, scorn contemporary public taste, forego the sale of his work and submit himself entirely to the judgment of posterity. (We have good reason to believe that this happened very rarely in the eighteenth century.) If, on the other hand, an architect wishes only to please himself, his plans will never leave the drawing-board. There are no monuments whose plans have not first been approved by a patron who has examined them and preferred them to other plans before committing himself to any expenditure. As in previous centuries, the history of architecture in the eighteenth century is the composite outcome of a gradual evolution in artistic form and in inventive ingenuity and of the desires and will of the monarchs (or of the wealthy —nobles, self-made commoners—who imitated the princes on a lesser scale). The life of artistic forms is here inseparable from the intentions formulated by the patrons; and, in their turn, these intentions are inseparable from the social, political and psychic context of the age.

LUXURY AND OSTENTATION

Building palaces for his court, his ministers, his mistresses; avenues in which to parade his coaches or his guards; theaters for his entertainment; industries to increase his income; churches in which to demonstrate allegiance to his God—the monarch of the seventeenth and eighteenth centuries acted as a being with unlimited needs. Buildings constructed "by order of the king" were essentially buildings "for the king." If he constructed a town—as Louis XIV's Versailles or Peter the Great's Petersburg—it was primarily to use it as his capital or his residence. Royal patronage meant that the king himself was the prime recipient of the works he had commissioned: he wanted them to reflect his greatness, to be a tangible representation of his power; and in fact everything displayed his crest, devices, ciphers, hereditary arms, images of his subjects' obedience. If he went in for buildings—as a victim of the "building mania" spoken of by Catherine II—they were occasionally practical instruments for new policies, but they were always meant to be visible, omnipresent proofs of the magic efficacy of his personal desires. An absolute monarch could hardly live under the roof of his forbears without adding new apartments to affirm tangibly the individuality of his own reign. But this "narcissistic" relationship between the prince and his own accomplishments became almost instantly an outward public act, a visible demonstration of sovereignty. In this respect the eighteenth-century monarchs, down to the tiniest German courts, were following an ostentatious Baroque tradition. But the outward show, at least in its older form, was more than mere show: it was a spectacle whose spectators were not to remain distant and objective; their freedom was lost in the captivating magic of the scene; they were systematically bewitched into participation, into a ritual submission, in a magnificent demonstration of the monarch's irresistible will. The ostentation was not simply the sign of sovereignty: it was the expression of power externalized, made perceptible to the senses, able to renew its outward manifestations indefinitely. The solemn image of the prince in the glory of his finery, exalted in his estates and palaces, demanded universal recognition. The personal relationship between the monarch and his domains was visible to the whole world: according to the myth of absolute power, the perception of this expansive glory should immediately transform the observer into a grateful subject, making him an integral element in the circle of royal possessions. Thus the relationship between prince and court was as between possessor and possessed; and this constituted the analogical image of the relationship the prince desired between himself and the entire world.

After the disturbances of the Fronde and the execution of Charles I, sovereigns were obscurely aware that they must thwart an undefined but deadly opposition: their ostentation was simultaneously an act of defiance and of protective magic. Though belief in divine right was unshakable in men like Louis XIV, the eighteenth century saw the gradual disintegration of the tacit and unstable solidarity between the authoritarian king and the bemused subjects, based on royal conviction and popular submission. The military defeats of the Roi Soleil, the scandals of the Regency, the installation of the house of Orange on the throne of England marked the beginning of an age during which the ritual and majesty of the monarchy were to be supplanted by mere pretense. Both the prince and his entourage regarded ceremonial as a convention, an artifice, and not as the magic creation of an absolute order; it was dominated by a spirit of play-acting. Far from imparting any genuine prestige, this frivolous ostentation merely embarrassed and encumbered the administrative services of the court, which constituted a separate world, isolated from the court yet dependent on it. The monarch's absolute authority could no longer be respected—in an age when the whims of a mistress could precipitate the dismissal of ministers and high officials. In a word, the central authority of the monarch ceased to be a dynamic driving force in the state. From this time onwards, court ceremonial was no longer a symbol of the monarch's far-reaching influence and will: it had degenerated into a meaningless, unjustified spectacle. The ostentation was devoid of real political significance: the king seemed to be a bored man seeking refuge from his lassitude by hearing operas, hunting, changing mistresses; the buildings he had constructed to this end, or for more serious purposes, did have a certain majesty, but their attraction and ornamentation suggested that the king's private pleasure took precedence over the public interest. Ordinary men and women, far from being captivated, charmed, drawn into a sense of collective admiration, felt increasingly that this was a world apart, from which they were excluded, a brilliant society whose wastefulness was ruining the nation. "It is almost impossible to be happy in Paris," wrote Sébastien Mercier, "because the rich pursue their haughty pleasures under the very eyes of the poor." At precisely the moment when architectural forms were becoming so harmonious—at the hands of architects immersed in the atmosphere of classical purity—the princely world behind these fine façades emerged as an independent, privileged, vainglorious world, concerned solely with the selfish pursuit of pleasure in its own private wonderland. This was the epitome of the narcissistic, overweening aspect of the Baroque—which repudiated the Baroque "rhetoric of persuasion," or else transformed this rhetoric into incoherent nonsense or speeches consisting merely of highflown facile clichés. (We must nevertheless acknowledge that architects in the first half of the century of Enlightenment were more successful than the French poets, who merely copied seventeenth-century classical tragedy.) Traditional forms became artificial, easy to handle because of long use, empty of substance; for although the age reveled in sensual forms these were merely symbols of wealth in conventional media. Luxury was little more than the decorative manifestation of the superfluous possessions of the rich which they wished to show off publicly.

Until the generation of Boullée and Ledoux the century was relatively uninventive in the forms of its exterior architecture, which was characterized by a dexterous reinterpretation of classical principles. The century made its mark primarily in interior decoration. Hedonistic conceits required an increase in enthusiasm and imagination from designers of wainscoting and paneling, as from cabinet-makers, goldsmiths, tailors, hairdressers, cooks... When ostentation aims at personal enjoyment rather than political influence it is evident that a person's immediate possessions (clothes, furniture, jewelry, curios, the décor of intimate rooms) take on added importance. At the same time fashions are bound to change very quickly, because tastes based primarily on the criterion of pleasure demand constant variety, surprises, originality. For the privileged, the artificial surface existence (which Rousseau calls "the arts" and we call "culture") became increasingly fine and complex, multifarious and evanescent, teeming with dainty knick-knacks, delighting in the slanting play of light in mirrors or polished surfaces. The sense of artificiality became still sharper as the rising bourgeoisie, eager to show itself off to advantage, tried to give expression to its prosperity by imitating the court. The bourgeois who had just made his fortune was akin to the aristocrat who had nothing left *but* his fortune. Of the great merchants for whom Watteau painted, Pierre Francastel has written accurately: "They are bourgeois who want not only power but culture; they want to influence society around them, wishing to rise in the social spheres where they were born and vaunt their success. As always, a revolutionary spirit compromises for a long time with the society which it finally destroys." Enriched financiers and traders became peers, acquired estates and titles, assumed a mask of nobility. Their superficiality and whimsicality is brought out by the glaring discrepancy between the minute calculation needed for gaining wealth and their pretense of aristocratic disregard for expenditure. Thus, whereas the genuine noble tends to restrict his pleasures to himself, the self-made parvenu tries to hide his origins by assuming an openly noble way of life; while his real aim is financial profit, he wants to resemble the noble who ruins himself in the name of honor or pleasure. In the event, the absolute monarchy—in France at least—was itself partly responsible for this evolution: by repressing the political pretensions of the old feudal nobility, who were so often hard to control, the king reduced them to the position of landowners verging on extinction who merely supplied him, at his own whim, with courtiers and officers. Montesquieu, representing the small provincial nobility, defined accurately what he considered to be the deplorable effects of Louis XIV's policy: the monarchy, he said, "particularizes everyone's interests." Civil architects constructed residences for the monarch or offices for his administrators (sometimes hospitals and churches); otherwise they used their talents to build private mansions, small châteaux, follies outside the bounds of the towns. Building contractors had to provide principally for the private interests of the wealthy on whom fortune had smiled.

Now fortune in the eighteenth century was if anything capricious: servants, farmers, charlatans, all were favored. They knew how to get their way, through honest crafts or underhand craftiness. The absolute monarchy was tolerant, often even welcoming, to the *nouveaux riches* who offered their services or bought lucrative offices. The hierarchical structure and corporation restrictions of the *ancien régime* were not so strict as to preclude absolutely the social advancement of talented men—or of agile adventurers.

Thus more and more representatives of a social power based exclusively on money (industry, commerce, finance) hastened to adopt the forms of an older social order, already very much weakened, and based on royal service and the protection of the people. Paradoxically, some of the bourgeois who had made their wealth by successful investments seemed to be avid to spend it as quickly as possible, copying the lavish expenditure and parasitic osten-tation that had been the prerogative of the courtier. They went in for masks. They tried to reach their particular ends while speaking a language which, socially, was not their own. In the declining feudal order whose historical basis of royal service, though ostensibly intact, had degenerated into an excuse for pleasure-seeking, it was not difficult for the rising bourgeoisie to adopt the way of life of the old privileged classes. "The wealthy are born to spend exorbitantly," wrote Voltaire. This is the point of view of a commoner turned aristocrat, who devoted much of his genius to managing his fortune; but others, whose moral values were stricter, or who had a clearer idea of their own interests, opposed this wanton luxury. The middle-class reaction against the spirit of the eighteenth-century aristocrats was defined appositely by the economist J. B. Say at the beginning of the following century. He set out "to explain the atmosphere of misery that surrounds the courts, where the greatest possible consumption takes place in the shortest time: the consumption of personal services, which are produced and consumed simultaneously. The services consumed are military, domestic, bureaucratic (whether useful or useless)—soldiers, servants, clerks, lawyers, clergymen, actors, musicians, society buffoons... Even material produce seems especially prone to destruction: fine foods, magnificent clothes, fashionable works of all kinds vie with one another for access to the court: nothing, or almost nothing, comes out again."

A JUBILANT BAROQUE

Spreading to Germany, Bohemia and even Russia, the Baroque style, with characteristic suppleness, adapted itself easily to the requirements of different times and places. The transition from Baroque to Rococo proceeded smoothly, by way of an intermediary style which might best be described as a "jubilant Baroque." Though it has lost something of the energy of high Baroque, it has already acquired the dramatic agility of Rococo and a hint of its decorative gaiety.

The Counter-Reformation, uncertain that people could always perceive the divine presence unaided, began to rely systematically on artistic representation. To win back souls to the faith, all the resources of pictorial rhetoric were brought to bear in highly emotional scenes showing the sudden incursion of the sacred into daily life. At Weltenburg, Cosmas Damian Asam designed a spectacular setting for St George's victory over the dragon; like the finale of a grand opera, it is a tableau inviting the onlooker's complicity. The rich display of colors, the skillfully contrived lighting focused on the silver horseman, the contagious undulation (which not only embraces the dragon, the knight's sword and the body of St Margaret, but follows the columns in their upward thrust), the slight obliquity of the general movement— all this combines to create an arresting effect of illusion. The whole place becomes an event, the space an emotion.

The profusion of colors and the strenuous movements of the caryatids, half disengaged from the massive pillars, make the library of the monastery of Metten resemble a magic grotto. Under these vaulted ceilings, where scenes from ecclesiastical history are surrounded by mythological putti *and stucco garlands, the universe of religion becomes a world of wonders. But the ineffable joys of faith are celebrated in the interior of the pilgrimage church of the Vierzehnheiligen, with its subtle counterpoint of superimposed circles and ovals. Here, around the central altar dedicated to the fourteen saints from which the church takes its name, Balthasar Neumann has created a buoyant upsurge of mingled gold, pink and white. The ceiling painted in* trompe-l'œil *opens a window on the infinite.*

COSMAS DAMIAN ASAM (1686-1739) AND EGID QUIRIN ASAM (1692-1750). ST GEORGE AND THE DRAGON, 1717.
MONASTERY CHURCH, WELTENBURG, BAVARIA.

F.J. HOLZINGER (1691-1775).
THE MONASTERY LIBRARY, METTEN, BAVARIA, 1706-1720.

BALTHASAR NEUMANN (1687-1753).
THE PILGRIMAGE CHURCH OF VIERZEHNHEILIGEN, FRANCONIA.

GIAMBATTISTA TIEPOLO (1696-1770). MOUNT OLYMPUS, CEILING FRESCO OF THE GRAND STAIRCASE, 1753. BISHOP'S PALACE, WÜRZBURG.

THE ROCOCO STYLE

In the eighteenth century luxury was a hybrid phenomenon, a temporary social union of the old and the new: the trappings of ostentation with which the divine-right monarchy had tried to dazzle its subjects into submission had degenerated into pure hedonism; material comfort and well-being became ends in themselves, entirely dissociated from the former invisible feudal order which had used wealth as a mere symbol. In the seventeenth century ostentation could still be the emblematic demonstration of the "charism" of the royalty or nobility. In the eighteenth century objects of luxury were merely the tangible presence of wealth converted into goods: their magnificence had no spiritual significance whatsoever; they were no longer the diffracted expression of an authority radiating throughout the world of appearances. (The pompous, devaluated survival of a form attached to a bygone order is nowhere more evident than in eighteenth-century tragedy, until the innovations of Diderot and the *Sturm und Drang*.) Luxury in the eighteenth century took advantage of the various forms (modified a little) in which authority had previously been voiced; but these forms now signified no hing beyond themselves; they no longer corresponded to their original context—and the artist could play with them capriciously for the sake of pleasure and variety.

For example, heraldic scrolls, traditionally intended for mottoes or devices, would be left blank, at the artist's disposal, twisted into elegant patterns and arabesques and surrounded liberally by prolific complex motifs: the scroll had entirely lost its emblematic function and had become mere background ornamentation. The disappearance of the symbolic element caused a corresponding profusion of lines and patterns, and with the absence of meaningful content the observer was left with superfluous decoration whose gratuitousness he might find either enthralling or scandalous. The form communicated no message; it was its own end. In this there was both weakness and excess: any underlying sense had evaporated more or less completely and the turmoil of sensual forms appeared overexuberant to the rational observer solely concerned with the requirements of utility and comfort. Therefore there is a distinct correlation between a social phenomenon and the aesthetic climate. To the enriched bourgeoisie, aping aristocratic manners, there correspond useful artistic forms (including scientific instruments, microscopes, compasses, etc.) enveloped by, and in a sense breeding, superfluous pseudo-artistic ornamentation; and to the aristocracy, dispossessed of its original functions, reduced to an unstable dependence on incomes from their estates and to the insecurity of sinecures, there would correspond the degeneration of artistic forms from symbolism to hedonism.

The Rococo style was prefigured at the end of the seventeenth century by Bérain, an expert in arabesque forms, and by Lepautre, the designer of the *Bâtiments du Roi*; it was developed by Oppenord and Vassé; and culminated in the asymmetric "picturesque" style of Pineau, Meissonnier and Cuvilliès. The Rococo style (Rococo is a general term including both the *style rocaille* and the *style Louis XV*) could be defined as a flamboyant Baroque in miniature: it crackles and flickers and scintillates, making the mythological images of authority childlike and effeminate. It is the perfect illustration of a form of art in which a weakening of underlying meaningful values is combined with an expansion of elegant, ingenious, facile, smiling forms—such forms as the high Baroque of the seventeenth century had, with its great theatrical gesture, intended to impart a full sense of authority. This art abounded in cherubs, garlands, arrows, quivers, seashells—shimmering pearl symbols of intimacy, with fan-like ribs and gently rounded, festooned edges; these were considered a suitably suggestive decoration for chimneypieces. The Rococo masked, rounded, softened the hard outlines of constructions with stuccoes and wainscoting, skillfully combining cosy intimacy with an agreeable sense of giddy movement.

A more demanding public, less attached to majestic dignity, insisted that their homes should be gayer, lighter, less spacious and therefore easier to heat. Louis XV himself followed this fashion: to the pomp and majesty of large halls he preferred the intimacy and convenience of more restricted, warmer rooms: the *petits appartements*. The Italian Milizia, at the end of the century, praised the convenience of French living quarters, where smaller rooms seemed to offer many advantages over the long series of vast suites that made Italian palaces so magnificent but so difficult to live in. "On the other hand, the exteriors of French buildings are neither so beautiful nor so impressive as ours; but it may never be possible to combine outside magnificence with inside comfort." This restriction of living space was accompanied by a proliferation of tiny ornaments: Chinese curios, decorative porcelain ornaments, sweetmeat boxes, snuff-boxes, miniatures.

Throughout Europe the vogue for fairy tales, sometimes metamorphosed into libertine tales, was part of the climate of deliberately cultivated childishness: the affectation of a nursery-like ingenuousness was an essential accompaniment of the Rococo mind. The stylist will notice how often English, French and German works of fiction have characters whose names incorporate the letter Z, reinforced by K or Ph. Z is an exotic letter for us, producing effects that may evoke antiquity (Zephyr), the Orient, fairyland, eroticism: Zaïre, Zélide, Tanzaï. "Zirziphile," whom we meet in Diderot's *Les Bijoux Indiscrets*, associates the seductions of the exotic letter with a childlike repetition of syllables (this applies also to the names of the heroes of the story, Mangogul and Mirzoza).

Sinuosity, which is one of the constituent elements of the Rococo, had its theorists, just as it was very quickly to have its critics. As a principle of art, it was advised initially for large pictorial compositions. In his *De arte graphica* (1688) Alphonse Dufresnoy defined it perfectly in Latin: "The parts must have waving contours, like a flame or a wriggling snake. The contours shall flow loose and vast, almost imperceptible to the touch." In 1700 Antoine Coypel used the same terms: "In the representation of figures... it is an elegance of form, vague and uncertain, waving and flickering like a flame, that imparts the sense of their animating spirit." In William Hogarth's *Analysis of Beauty*, the universal condition for grace and beauty is the undulating line. Beauty is derived from "the composed intricacy of form" with the power to "lead the eye in a kind of chase." An imaginary ray, leading from the eye, is drawn into a continuously varied movement: the variations enable us to escape from the dullness of repose; the continuity imposes order on the variety. In this endless movement the observer is never disorientated or bewildered. This is the pleasure inherent in tracing the path of these waving or serpentine lines: a pretty curl of hair, a ribbon entwined round a staff. The pleasure is increased, says Hogarth, when the object is in motion: "I can never forget my frequent strong attention to it, when I was very young, and that its beguiling movement gave me the same kind of sensation then, which I since have felt at seeing a country-dance; though perhaps the latter might be somewhat more engaging; particularly when my eye pursued a favorite dancer, through all the windings of the figure, who then was bewitching to the sight, as the imaginary ray, we were speaking of, was dancing with her all the time."

In many passages Hogarth tends to limit himself excessively to the pure geometry of the spiral; but here he confesses the erotic origin of his taste for the sinuous line. The grace and dignity of the undulation suggest the swaying movement of a dancing form and so reveal its feminine essence.

IGNACIO VERGARA (1715-1776). FAÇADE OF THE PALACE OF THE MARQUIS DE DOS AGUAS, VALENCIA (1740-1744),
DESIGNED BY HIPÓLITO ROVIRA Y BROCANDEL.

IMAGINATIVE DECORATION

The bold inventiveness of eighteenth-century decorators aroused criticism almost at once; in the name of enlightened taste this boldness was condemned for its resemblance to Gothic decoration. This judgment is unfair, but the comparison is by no means fortuitous. The palace of the Marquis of Dos Aguas at Valencia, which combines a number of influences, recalls Flamboyant Gothic, though at the same time it anticipates Gaudi and the "modern style." It is of particular interest in showing that the principle of sinuosity, so characteristic of the Rococo, can be made to harmonize in turn with an ideal of massive plenitude and one of light and graceful efflorescence. Around the main entrance of the Dos Aguas Palace, the stone swells out into urns, Atlantes, serpents, fruits or apparitions of the Virgin.

Turning to interior decoration, we find an equally exuberant imagination at work, but it aims now at breaking down volumes: foliage, flags, wings, garlands, ribbons, the pages of a book, offered the artist thin, flexible surfaces which lent themselves to light, evanescent compositions full of interlacing patterns and ornamental openwork. Elaborate curves and undulations, on the gilded stucco (or on the relief work of Capodimonte porcelain), catch the light, are reflected in mirrors, and sparkle in the drawing rooms with an ever renewed play of broken gleams.

The charm of Chinese pictures did not lie in their exoticism alone. The Chinese example was a constant stimulus to fanciful invention, to the pursuit of irregular and asymmetrical forms (in the tradition of the "grotesques"), and to combinations of curves and sharp angles, of the sinuous and the pointed: the supple was blended with the brittle. The artists of the Rococo thus resorted to all that was strange and striking in their quest for new visual stimulants.

FRANÇOIS DE CUVILLIÈS THE ELDER (1695-1768). HALL OF MIRRORS OF THE AMALIENBURG, 1734. SCHLOSS NYMPHENBURG, MUNICH.

SMALL SALON OF CAPODIMONTE PORCELAIN, 18TH CENTURY. MUSEO NAZIONALE DI CAPODIMONTE, NAPLES.

TAPESTRY WITH CHINOISERIES, 1730. SOHO FACTORY (?). WOOL AND SILK.
COLLECTION OF S.K.H. ERBGROSSHERZOG NIKOLAUS HERZOG VON OLDENBURG, GÜLDENSTEIN (OSTHOLSTEIN).

FRANÇOIS BOUCHER (1703-1770). THE EMPEROR OF CHINA GIVING AUDIENCE, 1742. MUSÉE DES BEAUX-ARTS, BESANÇON.

1

VARIETY IN DECORATION

It is true that the eighteenth century witnessed the ascendancy of French taste throughout Europe. At Schönbrunn, at Sans-Souci, in Stockholm and even in Russia, Versailles was taken as a model: men tried to adapt the architectural magnificence of the Roi Soleil to the celebration of new regimes outside France. But we should not allow this preponderance of French taste to blind us to the true originality of the Italian Baroque at the height of its maturity, to the particular spirit of the English empiricists, to the genius of the Churrigueras in Spain, or to what is specifically Germanic in the designs of such men as the Asams, Prandauer, Pöppelmann, Balthasar Neumann or the Dientzenhofers.

When he designed the pilgrimage church of Vierzehnheiligen for the Cistercians, Balthasar Neumann combined the principles of Italian Baroque and the French concept of order and proportion, adapting them to the Franconian landscape. To assemble vast crowds of people and stimulate their religious fervor, he constructed a basilica with a lofty façade whose curves and counter-curves recall the manner of Borromini. With its soaring height, its solid lines and the fluent rhythm of its twin towers crowned with bulbs and lanterns, this magnificent building is not simply one of the peaks of European art: it is also a reminder that at a time when large sections of the aristocracy and the middle classes were moving away from Christianity, the spirit of the Counter-Reformation still persisted, particularly in the center of Europe, in Southern Germany and Austria. In a style which sometimes tended to lack solemnity and was later inclined towards the insipid, this was the continuation of the movement that had begun with the Council of Trent and was to find its supreme expression in the Masses of Mozart and Haydn.

Beside their house at Munich the Asam brothers built a chapel for their private devotions, the church of St John Nepomuk. This lofty, narrow church, with its gallery of lively, undulating lines, illustrates, as Nikolaus Pevsner has pointed out, "the combination of strictly architectural composition and optical illusions to achieve an intense sensation of surprise which may easily turn into religious fervor." While here the suggestion of movement conveyed by the spiral columns and the effects of "transparency" may justify us in describing this as a work in the Baroque spirit, we find another type of Baroque in the work of Filippo Juvarra who aimed to captivate the observer by means of breadth of vision rather than by the suggestion of movement. Juvarra was a pupil of Fontana; he studied in Rome and worked as an architect and decorator in Piedmont, in the service of the House of Savoy. His style is marked by a rather harsh vigor combined with a highly developed feeling for "pictorial" effect. The shooting-lodge (Reale Fabrica) of the Stupinigi Palace near Turin, based upon a magnificent central plan, has four wings extending from the main body of the building in the form of a cross. While Scipione Maffei commended the skill with which each room was made to answer to its purpose, Milizia was less indulgent and held that Juvarra showed little regard for unity in his compositions, which, he said, were inelegant and unacceptable. Milizia's disapproval, expressed in the name of the Neoclassical ideal, was even sharper when turned against the exponents of the *Style Louis XV*. Oppenord is disposed of succinctly: "Oppenord is the French Borromini; his taste for extravagant outlines should be rejected in its entirety."

The leaders of the reaction which gained force in the 1750's heaped ridicule on the sinuous forms and the "capricious" style of such artists as Pineau, Cuvilliès and Meissonnier. The indictments made by Le Camus in 1780 are revealing: "We cannot regard as legitimate ornamentation these formless Baroque masses which lack any definition: they are mere 'flummery' *(chicorée)*. We must discard these Gothic eccentricities, even though they were still in use as recently as ten years ago and had, I fear, been current in France for over thirty-five years. It seems incredible that a type of art which owes its existence solely to a disordered imagination should have found favor among us. Perhaps we were led astray by a craving for novelty, perhaps also because it demanded so little effort to create objects in the Baroque style. Any form was acceptable; provided it twisted and flickered, all was well; harmony, symmetry, coherence, all were eliminated. You had merely to distort moldings hideously and counterbalance them with an apology of an escutcheon turned upside down and treated in the Rococo spirit, and your work would be hailed as a masterpiece..." This indictment was made to include Watteau and similar painters. Yet there is no denying that certain artists who now emerged as champions of a more formal genre and a more forceful, more disciplined style of ornamentation had begun by indulging in the asymmetry and wild sinuosity of the Rococo. Thus Piranesi's *Caprices* are drawn with the lithe freedom of natural plant growth; there is not the slightest hint that he was, later, to model his decorative style on the hieratic figurations of Egyptian art. This is simply one instance amongst many of the diversity of the experiments undertaken at this time. It is a warning against absolute classifications and rigid divisions into historical "periods."

VARIETY IN DECORATION

1. Balthasar Neumann (1687-1753): The Pilgrimage Church of Vierzehnheiligen, near Bamberg. Begun in 1743.

2. Filippo Juvarra (1676-1736): Oval Salon of the Stupinigi Palace, near Turin. Finished in 1733.

3. Cosmas Damian Asam (1686-1739) and Egid Quirin Asam (1692-1750): Interior of the Johann-Nepomuk-Kirche, Munich, 1733-1746.

4. Gilles-Marie Oppenord (1672-1742): Arabesque.

5. François de Cuvilliés (1695-1768): Caprice.

6. Juste-Aurèle Meissonnier (1675-1750): Ornament, 1734.

7. Giambattista Piranesi (1720-1778): Wash Drawing for an Urn.

8. Johann Bernhard Fischer von Erlach (1656-1723): Schönbrunn Palace, Vienna, 1691. Altered by Pacassi, 1744-1749.

9. Georg Wenceslaus von Knobelsdorff (1699-1753): Palace of Sans-Souci, Potsdam, 1745-1747.

ORDER AND VARIETY

The fashion immediately had its detractors and met resistance. Even those who followed the fashion would make fun of it. The Rococo delighted in satirizing its own creations. The mode of decorating relatively small interiors with a wealth of elaborate, gay detail must not be mistaken for the single determining characteristic of the style of the age. From the theoretical works of the time (bearing in mind the inevitable discrepancy between theory and practice) we learn that the proliferation of interior decorations corresponds to a pursuit of *variety* in order to balance the monotony that could result from the indispensable hegemony of *order*. The Rococo system is that of an authoritarian order tempered by asymmetry and by an increase in the complexity of detail, in the number of minute surprises. Thus in his *Essai sur le Goût* Montesquieu balances the complementary propositions. "It is not enough just to show the mind many things; they must be shown with order." But soon afterwards: "If order is necessary in things, so also is variety: without this the mind languishes... The soul must be shown things it has never before seen; the feelings imparted to it must be different from the feelings it has just experienced." At the same time the variety itself had to remain clearly visible and distinct, which is why the variety of Gothic art, considered to be chaotic, displeased Montesquieu together with most of his contemporaries. The critics of the *style rocaille* with its swarming abundance of decoration refer constantly to the danger of a resurgence of Gothic disorder. In this connection the Père André wrote: "It is not that there is insufficient art in this accumulation of tiny architectonic figures—there is too much; and nature, which makes do with less, will always reprove a profusion which satiates without satisfying."

Nothing is of value without symmetry—to which we must add contrasts and the unexpected. The rule which the age always invokes is pleasure of the soul: the dominant pleasure of observing symmetry; and the pleasure of perpetual renewal, in variety and contrasts. To explain this Montesquieu had recourse to the psychology of Locke: "Everything tires us in the long run, particularly the great pleasures: we leave them always with that same satisfaction with which we approached them... Our soul is weary of sensation; yet without sensation we should fall into overwhelming prostration. Anything may be remedied if we play on these modifications. If the soul has sensation, it does not weary. The particular disposition of the soul which leads it continually towards different objects causes it to delight in all the pleasures that come from surprise. Surprise pleases the soul both by the spectacle itself and by the promptitude of the action, for the soul notices or feels something which it did not expect or in a way it did not expect."

Order and variety: this was a reasonable theory, so reasonable that it could be held by schools which did not practise the same art. The Rococo stressed the abundance of variety in decoration, without in theory compromising in any way the predominant order of the general design. More demanding minds were later to be shocked by the audacious excesses of capriciousness and asymmetry of the Louis XV style designers. Caylus and Cochin, not to speak of the Englishmen whom Burlington converted to Palladianism, had nothing but scorn for the disorder and frivolous ornamentation of men like Cuvilliès or Meissonnier. A study of their writings reveals surprisingly that the opponents of the "picturesque style" include poets and artists whom we should have expected to be representatives of the Rococo.

After his journey to Italy, and no doubt encouraged by Madame de Pompadour, Cochin, the designer of Louis XV's *menus plaisirs*, undertook the defense of the "grand style" and set himself up as an opponent of mannerism and tortuous calligraphy. In an ironical *Supplication aux orfèvres* he wrote: "Goldsmiths are requested, when on the lid of a silver tureen they fashion a head of celery or an artichoke of natural size, to refrain from putting in beside them a hare as tiny as your finger... not to alter the destination of things, and to remember that a candlestick should be straight and vertical, to hold the candle... that a candle-ring should be concave to receive the dripping wax and not convex to make the wax run all over the candlestick. Sculptors of suites are requested to be pleased, when executing trophies, not to make a scythe smaller than a sand-glass, a man's head smaller than a rose... We shall then be able to hope at least that when things can be square craftsmen will be kind enough not to distort them; and that when copings can be semicircular they will refrain from deforming them with the S-shaped contours that they seem to have picked up from their writing masters... We beg them to bear in mind that we provide them with good straight pieces of wood and that they ruin us with high costs when they work them into these sinuous forms; and when they bend our doors to subject them to the round surfaces which they are pleased to give our rooms this makes us spend much more than if they were straight, besides which we can go through a straight doorway just as easily as through a rounded one. As for the curvature of the walls in our apartments, the only convenience this offers is to prevent us knowing where to place our chairs and other furniture." This refusal was of course formulated in the name of the same ideal of order and variety that Cuvilliès and Meissonnier themselves desired, but in order to satisfy both the eye and the mind it demanded a different standard of order, a different criterion of variety.

Not an excess of order, however. In expounding his ideas on the embellishment of towns, the Abbé Laugier, the theorist of the anti-Rococo reaction, did not argue for the perfect regularity which the spellbound Utopian architects were to propose. He wanted the rational order of avenues to be counterbalanced, as in a park, by a certain disorder which would reveal, if not a perfectly free nature, at least a great degree of decorative fantasy: "From time to time let us abandon symmetry and throw ourselves into the bizarre and the singular." A park is a forest submitted to the laws of art. The ideal city is a forest-town transformed into a park-town: "One should consider a town as if it were a forest. The essential beauty of a park arises from the multiplicity of its roadways, their width and alignment; but this alone is not sufficient: someone like Le Nôtre should draw up the plan, with taste and after reflection, and the park should show simultaneously order and oddness, symmetry and variety... No town but Paris provides the teeming imagination of an ingenious artist with such scope. Paris is a vast forest, varied by inequalities of plain and hill, divided by a great central river... Let us suppose the artist is allowed to cut and trim as he pleases—what immense advantages he could draw from such diversity!" The models that this opponent of the *style rocaille* took from the art of gardening, with the aim of applying them to the large towns, were the fine, embroidery flower-beds of seventeenth-century France: and paradoxically it seems to have been precisely these designs that inspired the creators of the Rococo style. The lessons of such statements as these do not concern only the history of taste: they reveal a turn of mind which belongs to the age as a whole. Faithful to the severe, virile canons of the art of antiquity, anxious to return to the refined forms of Roman architecture, our theorist appears to be by no means an innovator; on the contrary his admiration for the past allows us to define him as a conservative mind. But what airy, carefree Utopianism this conservative displayed when dealing with the wholesale transformation of a capital! The town, the product of a long history, was treated like a forest, in other words like an expanse of untamed nature upon which the innovating architect could impose at will, according to his own whims, avenues and squares and circuses of converging roads. It was suggested that Paris should be embellished, and immediately "rebuilding on a new plan" was proposed. What Wren had been unable to do after the fire of London, Laugier considered desirable for a town still intact. In fact, if like Patte we reproduce on a single map all the plans for squares and monuments in honor of Louis XV, we obtain the imaginary plan for a completely redesigned town. But these projects were not all carried out. The king deliberately refused to antagonize his subjects by destroying inhabited quarters in order to replace them by open spaces celebrating his own glory. The great spatial inventions of eighteenth-century Paris were sited on the periphery of the inhabited town: Place Louis XV (Place de la Concorde), Place de l'Etoile, Ecole Militaire... The great thoroughfares of the city (Laugier's "routes du parc") were not constructed until the nineteenth century: Laugier's project was an anticipation of Baron Haussmann's major reconstructions.

Laugier's proposals are therefore an extreme expression of the perfectly classical requirements of order and variety; their original aim—as would be the case for a real park—was simply to increase the pleasure of people out for a walk. Concern for utility was added to considerations of beauty: Laugier showed himself fully aware of the new demographic realities which were to necessitate modifications in the features of towns and their outskirts: "The entrance of a town is intended to assist the departure of inhabitants and the arrival of strangers... Everything should be quite free and unobstructed. The avenues contribute greatly to this freedom of access. By 'avenues' I mean the roads leading to the town: their width should be proportionate to the size of the population and concourse... The avenue should not simply be wide and as far as possible free of bends and detours; in addition the gateway and the corresponding internal street should have the same advantages. It would even be desirable that at the entrance to a large town there should be a large square, with a crossroads connecting with several streets. The entry into Rome by the Porta del Popolo is somewhat like this, and we have nothing similar in Paris." Thus the problems of access and function were stated in the clearest way possible, corresponding accurately to the rapid growth of the eighteenth-century capitals. But in practice these modern problems were to be handled in a language and style inspired from antiquity. In Laugier's theory, as in the great practicians of the second half of the century, boldness of intention was accompanied by an equal respect for the traditional forms of majesty. Sometimes, even, porches and columns were superadded, beyond any functional necessity, to buildings whose design was genuinely new. Audacity did not extend to dispensing entirely with the classical accessories. Hence in the closing years of the eighteenth century we find the same discordance between the "façade" and the contents which characterized both architectural design and the fashion of masks and disguises in the opening decades. Beneath an exterior of Baroque sumptuousness something was weakening, dwindling. Authority and power were no longer absolutely compelling. The façade, the railings were becoming the visible frontier of a totally unsacred domain given over entirely to pleasure. At the end of the century the affirmations of those determined to innovate were concealed under the appearances of the old order: this was precisely the period when the revolutionary ideology still had recourse to the outdated forms of classical tragedy, when the rhetoric of the Jacobins was clothed in the elegant formulae of Plutarch and Tacitus. Borrowings, masks, mythologies of a former age: these indicate a discrepancy between the mentality of the period and inventiveness in artistic form. The discrepancy would not have been so marked without the prodigious social and intellectual changes which made inherited forms fall into obsolescence while the forms themselves were still nostalgically retained. From this point onwards reflection could develop upon reality and appearance, the necessary and the superfluous, the natural and the artificial, energy and decadence. No age was more aware of the conventionality of its tastes, more curious about the changes it did not dare to introduce; no age was riper for experiment. A few bold minds did not hesitate to affirm that man is the author of his own history and that he is perhaps the creator of his values: everything that man is, and everything around him, can be changed by an act of his own will. And this discovery in itself, *ipso facto*, made everything change.

2

PUBLIC SQUARES
AND PRIVATE HOUSES

In towns where land is scarce public squares may seem an idle luxury, a waste of space, occupying lavishly the land which is apportioned niggardly to the average inhabitant. Space is a luxury. Consequently the public squares of the period were always "dedicated"—to kings, to saints, to victories, to allied nations.

In Paris, for example, the Place Louis XV (now Place de la Concorde) originated in this impulse towards "dedication," for it was constructed as a result of Bouchardon's commission in 1748 to set up a monumental statue to King Louis XV. This statue had to be sited in the most august and conspicuous position possible, and the first step was to clear and demarcate a vast open space in which the effigy of the king would nevertheless seem to be absolutely dominant. Rejecting proposals which would have involved the destruction of an inhabited area of the capital, the king decided to utilize a stretch of waste land between the Tuileries and the Champs-Elysées. "Gabriel, the architect who drew up the plan, had the idea of giving the new square a general design similar to the forecourts on which the avenues in château grounds converge. A wide ditch was dug around the esplanade, faced with walls and surrounded by a balustrade, with openings at intervals to provide ways of ingress. The space thus enclosed was divided up into railed-off lawns with carriage drives between them" (Marcel Poëte). Facing the palaces there were many trees and plantations of shrubbery: this is a good example of the interpenetration of town and country so much desired by the best minds of the century. But even this did not satisfy Diderot. He maintained that the architect should have shown more respect for the natural woodlands of the area: "Had I been asked to construct the Place Louis XV at its present site, I should have taken good care not to cut down the forest and so arranged things that one could glimpse its shadowy depths between the pillars of a great peristyle."

An architect cannot of course create out of nothing, allowing his imagination completely free play. Gabriel was granted space, and he managed to produce an impression of grandeur by setting up magnificent palaces which made the vastness of this space *perceptible*. At the Piazza di Spagna in Rome, on the other hand, the architect had far less scope; the square was already in existence, as was the church of Trinità dei Monti. As from the seventeenth century plans had been suggested, in keeping with the Baroque spirit, for combining the church and the square into an organic whole, the vital link being a monumental stairway. It was Francesco de Sanctis who achieved this result (the work was begun in 1725). A hitherto enclosed square, which had been virtually isolated from the outside world (resembling in this respect the Piazza Navona), now became an open space, presenting the spectacle of a breathtaking upward movement in which effects of depth and height were merged together.

The Hémicycle at Nancy combines a sense of monumentalism and of intimacy by means of its colonnade. Possibly—as Louis Hautecœur suggests —it is meant to recall the colonnade in St Peter's Square. In any case it acts as an organic link between the Palais du Gouvernement and a complex of buildings whose disposition is governed by an overall plan striking a harmonious mean between order and diversity. Turning from the Hémicycle at Nancy to the Royal Crescent at Bath we find a similar geometrical arrangement adapted to a different purpose; the Royal Crescent is not an ornamental colonnade surrounding an open "square," but an uninterrupted

series of dwellings looking out over a lawn. The architect, John Wood, succeeded in producing a striking impression of strength allied with grace. In addition, the Crescent suggests a sense of individual privacy which compensates for the spatial proximity of the dwellings. It is the architectural counterpart of the society described in the novels of Jane Austen: a combination of independence and interdependence in which human relationships gradually become so subtle and delicate that for the novelist they are the épitome of human complexity.

Was the residence of the wealthy man a small palace or a large villa? Too large a dwelling would have been a troublesome burden: he wanted trees and greenery and a garden in which he could relax and muse freely, away from the petty obligations of official or social functions. But he also needed elegance, harmony and a sense of imposing majesty. Gabriel's triumph with the Petit Trianon lay in the creation of an atmosphere of dignity without grandiloquence, of charm without affectation. The Petit Trianon is sumptuous and lively, combining order and dignity with a suggestion of intimacy.

Burlington drew inspiration from Palladio's country houses but he was not a slavish imitator. With Chiswick House, as Kaufmann has pointed out, Burlington "deviated from Palladio's models, both when he was more Baroque—as in the exceptional feature of the stairs and the lofty dome—and when he was less Baroque—as in the total composition and the garden-front window."

At the end of the century architects were still using the same vocabulary (colonnades, balustrades, porticoes, arcades and so on), but their meaning had already changed. In one of his earliest creations, the Hôtel de Brunoy, Boullée introduced columns that are more slender and give a greater illusion of height, and designed the roof in the form of a truncated pyramid crowned by a statue of Flora. Contemporary critics regarded this as the product of an excessive, overwrought imagination. In the château at Villadeati, with its agile series of terraces and galleries rising in contrasting curves, the regularity and harmony of classical architecture has been interpreted with a highly imaginative lyricism.

PUBLIC SQUARES AND PRIVATE HOUSES

1. Jacques-Ange Gabriel (1698-1782): Place Louis XV (Place de la Concorde), Paris. Print after Lespinasse.

2. Giambattista Piranesi (1720-1778): View of the Piazza di Spagna, Rome, 1750. Etching.

3. Germain Boffrand (1667-1754): The Palais du Gouvernement and the Hémicycle de la Carrière, Nancy, 1715. Completed by Héré de Corny, 1753-1755.

4. John Wood the Younger (1728-1781): The Royal Crescent, Bath, 1767-1775.

5. Jacques-Ange Gabriel (1698-1782): The Petit Trianon in the Park of Versailles, Garden Façade, 1762-1764.

6. Lord Burlington (1694-1753): Chiswick House, Chiswick, Middlesex. Begun in 1725.

7. Etienne-Louis Boullé (1728-1799): The Hôtel de Brunoy, Paris, façade giving on the Champs-Elysées, about 1774. Print.

8. The Castle of Villadeati, near Turin, late 18th century.

1

2

3

4

5

6

II

PHILOSOPHY AND MYTHOLOGY OF PLEASURE

THE PRIMACY OF SENSATION

The eighteenth century discovered all the problems inherent in pleasure, and this was much like actually inventing pleasure. It made pleasure as much an object of serious reflection as of frivolous experience, singling it out and making it unusually conspicuous. In the arts it suppressed or loosened the bonds of dependence that tradition had established between pleasure and rational discernment, between pleasure and edification of the soul. Scholars themselves now questioned the criteria of pleasure: morally, should pleasure always necessarily be the result of virtuous action? In art, must it necessarily be subordinated initially to inspection and judgment? Pleasure had previously taken second place; it was now to have precedence. Needing no justification itself, pleasure became the universal justification. The enjoyment that Poussin had spoken of was consecutive to an act of reason. But there was now arising a form of art whose pleasurable qualities were to be captured by immediate intuition, in a state of delectable uneasiness. "Sensibility, instead of being something negative, inferior, preparatory, was becoming essentially positive" (Victor Basch). Whatever the confusion of our response to a work of art, this is not simply an initial reaction, it is itself the decisive response. A theorist, the Père André, reproved this primacy of the senses in an excellent analysis: "When pleasure precedes a clear and distinct perception of the perfections of an object that strikes us, I acknowledge that this object pleases us, either because it affords us pleasure or as a result of the pleasure which it has intimated to us. This is the way in which objects perceptible to the senses arouse our appreciation: they are first sensed, before they are recognized... Thus they enter the heart under cover of darkness." But while the Père André believed that these objects "would lose immensely if examined in the light of reason," another theorist, the Abbé Du Bos, set out to justify the charm by which a beautiful work captivates one before any reflection whatsoever. The "decision of the sensations" precedes any reasoning: and reason will in fact intervene "in our judgment of a poem or of a picture in general, only to justify rationally the decision of the sensations, to explain what fault prevents it from pleasing or what attractions make it possibly engaging." The explanatory role devolving on the faculty of reason remains very important, but it is an auxiliary role, *a posteriori*. Reason comes, after the event, to justify the initial pleasure. According to the theorists there was no danger in this—for men of taste at any rate—since pleasures of the senses, by a kind of instinct, are aroused only by works or beings in which the reason will afterwards be able to find points of perfection. Similar opinions were voiced at the same period by moralists who believed they were not conceding too much in admitting that man was born for pleasure and happiness, adding immediately that only virtue was capable of assuring the most durable pleasures, the most constant happiness. By all means seek sensual pleasure, but do not ignore your long term interests! In this way morality meant both to renew its rights and to make itself attractive, recommending transient sensations but with an eye to permanent values.

This rivalry between judgment and sensibility was reconciled ideally in a theory of complex beauty: perfect harmony arises from the coexistence of order designed to satisfy the mind, and a variety of details and nuances capable of arousing the senses in agreeable surprise. Order and variety: these two principles of classical aesthetics were interpreted as qualities which would appeal simultaneously to both judgment and sensibility. With certain aspects of the work of art (symmetry, clarity, etc.), the judgment is given priority. With other aspects (ornamentation, charming oddities), pleasure results from an immediate startling impact.

Was eighteenth-century life a life of pleasure? At any rate, men thought about pleasure, which is not quite the same thing. Pleasure, the transitory reign of pleasure, these were the subject of debate, of reflection, of imaginative representation. The arithmetic of pleasure was worked out and when the last line had been drawn some men calculated that the sum of evils in life was greater than the sum of pleasures. So the works of art that men gathered around themselves tended to compensate for a lack, to capture through images an elusive ideal.

This rehabilitation of pleasure made luxury more easily justifiable and enshrined officially the values of this world and the untrammeled movement of an adventurous consciousness. In pleasure the individual asserts his primacy and looks upon himself as his own end.

The sociologist, analyzing the images and theories of pleasure, will note once again a curious ambivalence. For feudal societies, in which everything should be subject to God through the hierarchy of temporal suzerainties, the pursuit of pleasure is the sign of a certain dissolution. When a noble becomes a "voluptuary" and lives apart in his own pleasure, when his pleasures are no longer just an incidental pastime but come to constitute the sole end of his existence, the whole spiritual structure which justified the privilege of his rank is repudiated. The privilege becomes an abuse; race and blood become superstition; and in his flickering pleasures the solar myth of royalty disintegrates and fades away. For the well-to-do middle-class man, on the other hand, pleasure does not imply any neglect of duty or of his proper function. He regards pleasure as a right, through which he affirms the ruling passion inclining him towards worldly wealth. Self-love and a taste for pleasure were the first principles of a morality in which all things henceforth began with man himself (observed only by an abstract God and a bountiful Nature). Instead of being the residue of a fading power, pleasure was the basic phenomenon upon which a new conception of social life could be built. For this "principle of pleasure" purported to be expansive: it was maintained that pleasure was increased by being communicated, that it was always concerned with the happiness of others,

that it was compatible with effort and work. This was an additional reason why men, each in his own activity, should exchange lucrative services, under the benevolent protection of a government guaranteeing equality and security.

There is, therefore, no greater opposition than that between these two meanings of pleasure. In the first, we have the final revelries of the libertine who has said farewell to the "man of stone," a solitary, futureless ecstasy, stumbling against death, condemned to the numbness of repetition or the deadening mire of boredom: *Après moi, le déluge*. In the second, we find the original experience of a special asset which at first belongs to the individual, only to make him more clearly aware that it should be shared by everyone; no longer stigmatized as a sin, it has become the natural measure of the just and the unjust. Taken in this sense, pleasure is not dissipation; it is, on the contrary, linked with the awakening of the individual, it is the triumphant energy which enables the mind to understand itself, gather up its strength and dedicate itself to the world and to others. A few men, followers of Epicurus, even regarded pleasure as the sole authority that could be substituted validly for the outworn figures of Authority. "Indulge yourself—there is no other wisdom; have others indulge themselves—there is no other virtue" (Senancour).

If we simplified a little and attributed a particular mentality to each social group, we should distinguish a twilight pleasure, as at nightfall, prey to black despair (which would characterize the aristocratic mind), and an optimistic form of pleasure, "matutinal," prepared to enroll everything under the rule of law (which would be the ideal norm of the most emancipated section of the bourgeoisie). Both these aspects of pleasure show it to have been directed beyond itself, towards an end which was far from frivolous: for the first, it was the absolute nothingness which was increasingly to obsess the pre-Romantic "sentimentalists"; for the others, it was hope in a world reconstructed according to Nature and to Reason.

THE FICTITIOUS ASCENDANCY OF WOMAN

Woman reigned; that is, she was led to believe that she reigned. Around her there hovered the promise of pleasure. But the situation is ambiguous. For the few who were their own mistresses, who reigned over the salons by their wit and knowledge, how many others were treated as mere objects: locked away in convents, married against their will, tricked into submission. History teaches us, however, that the majority remained strictly confined within the household, occupied virtuously with their domestic duties. But it was not so in the chosen lands of wealth, where luxury abounded and art was a constant commodity. Whereas the terminology of passionate respect deluded women into believing that a man's whole destiny depended on their favors, the sole ambition of the suitor was in fact simply to *have* yet another woman. It is not surprising that in her turn woman soon masked herself and vied with man in hypocrisy: fine sentiments were now little more than the point of honor of sensual desire. Tender protestations were the code language of carnal impatience, the preliminaries by which the intelligence prepared the way for the overthrow of reason. A complete, highly refined system of mutual acts of consideration and respect, of exchanged compliments, letters and portraits, was brought into play in order to achieve with absolute certainty the tumult of animal satisfaction.

This refined language was therefore a mask, a "veil" which no one misconstrued, but which everyone made use of, because disguises and false obstacles held caprice in suspense. "The rest of my youth," affirms one hero of *Les Bijoux Indiscrets,* "was wasted away with such pastimes, always with women, women of every kind, seldom mysteriously, and with many solemn pledges, all quite devoid of sincerity." One would pledge an eternal love, but it was understood in advance that "the pleasure of love lasts but an instant." This implicit knowledge, usually shared by both lovers, did not prevent them from pouring out the vain formula of their pledge;

and the words were empty because nobody believed that the spoken word was binding for the future. This is a further example, now on the level of personal conduct, of the century's characteristic recourse to specious "façades." The deceiving externals dissimulated, but they let it be known that they were doing so. Elegant lies, having become a general convention, led to no misapprehension. They established a style, a manner of speech, in which the truths of real life and the contrivances of language developed alongside, but at a respectful distance from each other—elegant speech being simply the obligatory periphrasis (unless one indulged in the contrary affectation of a "fishwife" style).

The visual arts contributed to this recognized rhetoric of fiction. On the one hand, pictures had the express function of representing clearly those aspects of pleasure which decency forbade the written word. They stated aloud the facts that elegant language could only hint at. On the other hand, their aim was to deify sensual desire, to disseminate the obsession of desire under the garlands and celestial blues of an eternal spring. Thus art was given the function of being both daringly frank and subtly suggestive. In paintings for boudoirs, on overdoors and on piers between windows, Boucher and his imitators celebrated the glory of love through the apotheoses of a disguised mythology. Nothing is more real, since pleasure is universally acknowledged. Nothing is more false, since everything is transposed into the tone of a fable whose mythical origins are only perceptible in certain elements of the general presentation: in pretexts for poses, for interesting scenes, for eddying flights of Cupids. In this alluring world the novelties of pleasure seem to be inexhaustible and, since we are somewhere other than in real life, nothing will even breathe of lassitude or death.

Mythology offers a strange new background and, inherently, a plausible pretext, authorized by the poetic traditions, for displaying nakedness, abductions and embraces. Now this double function, which both reveals and mystifies, can be assumed by any entrancing phantasmagoria whatsoever. Any human interdiction may be by-passed if the imagination can be transported into a different element. Exoticism, which complements mythology, provides similar alibis: the mind frees itself of its prejudices, pretends to be other than it is, affects to be observing itself from without. By means of exotic ornamentation and background (even if these are quite false), sensuality escapes into a different moral universe, into an atmosphere in which its wishes may be fulfilled without too much resistance. In literature, exoticism was also used to disguise and quicken social satire: the scandals of the capital could be denounced under a thin veil of fiction that situated them in Laputa, or exposed them to the wonderment of a Persian. There is undeniably a perceptible natural bond between the masquerading which enlivens the darting relish of pleasure, and the disguises by which criticism too sharpens the tip of its shafts. Shafts of wit or Cupids' arrows: it is in the momentary sharp prick, the quick sting, the acute pain, in the ephemeral and the discontinuous that the century manifested its particular genius, between the old monumental order of the Baroque and the dreamy effusions of Romanticism.

The image of a strange universe, more than half invented, made possible an ironical liberation. Exoticism and mythology enable the mind to move back into the unreal, either to be intoxicated by it or to find in it the point of view from which reality may be described as a comedy. Before the century began to yearn for *genuine feeling*, it indulged in the delights of all the varieties of personal dissociation. Allegories, transpositions, antiphrases, double meanings, allusions: these were just so many mental experiments with the separateness, the obliquity that relieved the tensions of life, and made life agreeable in the unrest that inevitably marked the various spheres of elegant society: the court, the town, the salons... Romanticism itself first began to appear only when dissatisfaction—not simply a wandering curiosity—dictated genuinely new departures for places where the heart could be regenerated. For the men of the Rococo, exoticism was merely a new formal expedient: they removed to imaginary lands the degrading adventures which were topics of daily conversation in London or Paris. Without leaving home they enhanced the richness of their

familiar world with the perfumes and cloths of the colonies: waited on by little black servants, an Englishwoman could become a sultaness.

By the combined effects of the general state of mind and the decorative background, life took on the mobility of fiction, an air of entertainment. An agile rhetoric used all its ingenuity to indicate its object (or its lack of object) by means of *images of something else*. Thus people put on masks, with no intention of remaining masked; they openly paraded their insincerity. To this ambivalent rhetoric there corresponded symbolically the practice of leading a double life. The wealthy man had both wife and mistresses; town houses and country cottages. Although pleasure was scarcely clandestine at all, it did require its own sacred domain, its own favorable secluded territory: actresses, the virtuosi of dual personality, were predestined to live there. "Everybody kept a separate establishment," declares one of the characters in *Les Bijoux Indiscrets*. "I had one in the east suburb where I installed, one after the other, some of those women of the town, the kind you see for a time, then see no more, to whom you speak and yet say nothing, and turn away when they pall on you. There I brought together my friends and actresses from the Opera, and we had little parties which Prince Erguebzed sometimes honored with his presence. Ah, Madam, I had delicious wines, exquisite liqueurs, and the best cook in the Congo." This was eighteenth-century France (under the name of the Congo), but it was also the Opera, unmasked, because the Opera belonged already to the world of make-believe. The kingdom of pleasure, both homogenous and scattered far and wide, existed parallel to the real world. In a certain way it had its capital: the stage of the Opera. It had its temples: country follies. It opened on the external world: with fashionable avenues, gardens, wooded drives in which to strut and parade, rotundas for dancing, like the Palais Royal or the Vauxhalls. It had its altars and intimate décors: the boudoirs.

In 1780 a French architect, Le Camus de Mézières, conceived the arrangement of a boudoir in this way: "The boudoir is regarded as the abode of sensual delight, where plans may be meditated and natural inclinations followed. It is essential for everything to be treated in a style in which luxury, softness and good taste predominate... One should at all costs avoid the hard, crude shadows thrown by lighting that is too vivid. The light should be mysterious: this will be obtained by placing mirrors over part of the casements. Openings and repetitions may be produced in abundance by means of mirrors. But see to it that they do not form the bulk of the furnishings. Too many of them will make the room seem bleak and monotonous. They should be distributed in such a way that each is separated from the next by a space of at least twice the length of a single mirror. These restful intervals can be decorated with rich and beautiful fabrics, and in each such setting a picture can be artfully hung with thick tassels and silk cords plaited with gold thread. The subjects of the pictures will be taken from the loves of the gods. The triumph of Amphitrite, Cupid and Psyche, Venus and Mars, will provide themes well in keeping with the character of the place. Here all must be cosy, all must give pleasure. Details designed to be seen close at hand must be in perfect harmony with the room as a whole. Here the principal object is to bring together an unbroken succession of delights. If the casements are to the east, the light will be softer; as far as possible they should look out on favorable views; however, in the absence of Nature herself, have recourse to Art. This is where taste and genius should be displayed to the full; every resource must be brought into play, using the magic of painting and perspective to create illusions... The boudoir would be all the more delightful if the recess where the bed is placed were provided with mirrors; the joints could be concealed by carved tree-trunks, gathered skillfully in leafy masses and painted after Nature. The repetition would form a quincunx, multiplied in the mirrors. The visual effects would be enhanced by an arrangement of candles and gauze hangings, some stretched tightly, others floating loose, to produce a graduated light. The boudoir would seem like a grove of trees, and painted statues distributed appropriately would add to the charm and the illusion."

A counterfeit nature here creates a wonderful world of make-believe in which Flora, "decked in brightest colors, awaits in secret the endearments of Zephyr." But this remains a servile, mercenary art, intended merely to please and subject to the whims of the rich. A contemporary, the Comte de Caylus, deplored the state of bondage to which the artist was reduced but saw no hope of better things. "Those who patronize artists, whether grandees or rich men, are entitled at the very least to have a say in the work they order. But however right and natural may be their determination to have their way, it has often thwarted the best will in the world and checked the impulses of genius... The result of this state of affairs is to put the arts at a disadvantage which will often be their bane in times to come, as it has in the past. The mischief can only be undone by leaving the artist a free hand in the execution of his work, in all its parts." The same complaint had already been voiced in Italy. Were the artists of the following generations to be any more successful in claiming full freedom of invention and asserting the indefeasible rights of genius?

THE OLYMPUS OF THE CEILINGS

Inspiration remained Alexandrian until almost the end of the century. Classical mythology was reduced to charming and conventional fables peopled by nymphs and cupids. The gods of this art have nothing mysterious about them. What painters and sculptors sought to represent was not the essence of any awe-inspiring divinity, but merely the outward attributes assigned them by tradition—a repertory of attitudes, clothing and accessories chosen and arranged according to the requirements of the decoration. No sense of sovereign power or authority here, none in any case until the time of Winckelmann; these deities are young men and women of flesh and blood, pretexts for a display of brilliant colors and precious materials. Callimachus wrote of "golden-clad Apollo whose clasp, lyre, arrows and quiver, and even his shoes, are of gold, for gold befits the riches of this god." And Levesque comments as follows: "This idea of the poet should be borne in mind by the painter. Gold can be employed lavishly in the portrayal of Apollo, especially when he symbolizes the sun, because the bright color of the most precious of metals bears a close resemblance to the color of the sun." This advice was taken to heart by Boucher. We must not look to him for any sense of the supernatural; but what a profusion of glowing colors, what a happy blend of golden light with the tints of milky flesh!

It is these mythological scenes that give an air of make-believe and bustle to eighteenth-century residences. In the depths of the parks, around the fountains, and on the ceilings, the heroes and heroines of mythology create a world apart, a world of pleasing fancy and delightful illusions. The ceiling painter, writes Robin, "magnifies space by multiplying planes and affords us the pleasure induced by the movement and forms of a pleasing whole... A well-arranged ceiling painting gives life and movement to all parts of an interior which, otherwise, would be only a vast solitude. It comes as the crowning touch to all the adornments of the art of building... or as a bright garment whose luster quickens the ordinary forms of beauty."

FRANÇOIS BOUCHER (1703-1770). APOLLO REVEALING HIS DIVINITY TO THE SHEPHERDESS ISSÉ, 1750. MUSÉE DES BEAUX-ARTS, TOURS.

ANTONIO GUARDI (1698-1760) AND FRANCESCO GUARDI (1712-1793). DAWN, ABOUT 1750. PRIVATE COLLECTION, VENICE.

GIAMBATTISTA TIEPOLO (1696-1770). THE TRIUMPH OF APOLLO, CEILING FRESCO IN THE IMPERIAL HALL, 1752.
BISHOP'S PALACE, WÜRZBURG.

GIOVANNI BATTISTA PITTONI (1687-1767). DIANA AND ACTAEON. MUSEO CIVICO, VICENZA.

LUIGI VANVITELLI (1700-1773). THE FOUNTAIN OF DIANA. BEGUN IN 1752. PARK OF THE ROYAL PALACE, CASERTA, NEAR NAPLES.

REPRESENTATION

A play of mirrors: an art which aimed at dispensing pleasure by taking pleasure itself as its subject; paintings which sought to seduce by presenting scenes of seduction. The picture will please, provided that it depicts sensual pleasure. Writing about paintings for the decoration of the ideal boudoir, Le Camus notes that "the principal object is in a way the close juxtaposition of real and figurative enjoyment." Thus "happy moments" constituted the theme, the narrative content through which the artist wanted to arouse "agreeable emotions." Just as religious painters had wished to edify by producing countless pictures of acts of faith, the artists of pleasure, to defend and illustrate the Epicurean credo, depicted countless scenes of sensual delight. This amounts, once again, to propaganda through representation, but the propaganda was now based on the contagion of sensory pleasure, the realistic evocation of silks, skin texture, gazing and glancing eyes.

Gillot paints theatrical scenes, catching the postures and grins of the actors. De Troy, too, sets about representing a world which has itself already taken up an attitude of representation: he makes the courtiers and wealthy bourgeois pose for him in surroundings which are precisely those of elegant life—conversations, games, meals, etc. The play of appearances is raised to the second power in this set image of a life devoted to the pleasure of appearances. By imitating appearances, these paintings offer us the spectacle of a spectacle.

What gives De Troy and so many other painters of the period their "documentary" interest is that they take up a position not before natural forms, but before products of culture. The painter's art derives its pleasure from including in the picture a whole range of objects and figures which are themselves works of art: details of architecture, sculpture, furniture, silks, jewels, lace. De Troy was preceded by very many artists—from the noblest to the lesser

arts, from architect to wig-maker, from jeweler to bootmaker—before he even took up his brush! And these faces, these features were long composed in mirrors before the painter began to copy them for his own composition! All the arts of seduction see their functions preserved in the superior seduction of the picture which resembles them.

So the art of the painter duplicated a reality which had already been organized as a visible triumph of art. The *Enseigne de Gersaint*, in which the painter looks at personages looking at paintings, can be regarded as typifying this representation of representation. But in Watteau imitative duplication rose to the heights of the dream and of poetic invention. From the model—as so many drawings prove—he sought the secret of an attitude, the undulation of a dress, a special aspect of the nape beneath combed-up hair. His gift of style was so intense that in copying the fashion of the day he created the fashion of the morrow. And when he arranged the actors and lovers in leafy glades, he offered his century the example of a holiday-like festivity at once possible and improbable. Were these actors, these great ladies, these peasants really ever merged and mingled in this way? Where could such trust and tenderness be found outside Watteau's dreamworld? But by giving his personages fashionable clothes and hair styles, he suggested the immediacy of a golden age, the probability of a longed-for happiness. If these paintings were not the imitation of a real spectacle, they were at least an attractive, engaging image, a promise which could probably be fulfilled: the observer believed that he could easily be taken there. There is nothing, apart from the special light, the indefinable touch and the fleeting instant of grace, that could not be re-enacted immediately beneath the branches of a real grove. Despite a few flights of Cupids, the scene is not in Arcadia; Cythera is not in Greece; it is a section of the French countryside; further, it is a painter's horizon. By introducing an occasional clumsiness of form, distorting a nose, coarsening a smile, Watteau shows his desire to remain on a human level, to avoid constructing an imaginary paradise. Unlike the courtly portraitists he was reluctant to disguise his personages as mythological figures. More subtly he sets up, in the heart of his groves of trees, statues of pagan deities—Venuses, fauns, terminal gods—to witness discreetly the pleasures of which they are the deified figures. What is strange is the casual familiarity, half credulous, half allegorical, which unites mankind and the gods. The unreality is neither in the background nor in the figures, but in the characters' uncertain faith which causes them to pursue their pleasures with such seriousness. They live religiously in a universe of pleasure. The characters are paying religious homage, making a pilgrimage—to the apparent exclusion of everything that is not their own high emotion. Watteau's taste was normally for the intervals, the moments when eyes glance away, when the conversation stops, or when the musicians are tuning up: moments of interruption at which the heart is touched by an absence, unless it opens to a mysterious presence. Watteau's personages, with their hands together and their eyes straying away, offer the gods of pleasure the spectacle of their distraction. They steal away from the representation. In the *Pilgrimage to Cythera* the couples are moving away from the statue of Venus after bringing their offerings: homage has been paid, the statue will remain, alone. The melancholy of Watteau lies in this coexistence of a contemplative presence and a suggestion of withdrawal, of an immediate intimacy and a beckoning distance. It is the melancholy of an artist who is aware that his joy in painting replaces joy in living.

FÊTES GALANTES

"Isles, enchanted isles, separated from the land by a crystal ribbon!... Here under the trees, in an uncharted spot chosen at random, is everlasting indolence" (Jules and Edmond de Goncourt).

Enamored of nature and of acting, Watteau invented a new type of painting in which his actors not only play their parts in a natural setting but are blended with nature, while the distinction between the world of the theater and the world of fashion is effaced. Here invention prevails over imitation; the composition is suggested by dreams or memories. For Watteau builds up the picture by assembling a variety of scattered elements: lighting effects from Rubens, foliage from the Luxembourg gardens, figures from his sketchbooks. "He had certain fashionable clothes and some comedian's costumes," wrote his friend the Comte de Caylus, "in which he dressed up such persons as he could find, of either sex, who were willing to pose for him, and whom he portrayed in the attitudes that nature suggested... When the fancy took him to paint a picture, he turned to his collection of studies, choosing from it the figures best suited to his mood of the moment." But there is a world of difference between the histrionic poses in his studio and the elaborate setting worked out on the canvas "toning in with a landscape background." Far from being a mere stage-disguise, Mezzetin's costume has now become one with the man himself, perfectly attuned to the shadowy glade and the arpeggios of his guitar.

In Watteau's imaginary world, finery and fashionable dress are the outward signs of a desire to please and be liked, to charm and beguile. But woman, here, is as eager to dominate as she is to love. To become the unique object of desire is to possess a tyrannical power. But when there are so many rivals, who can be sure of retaining her conquests? Those who lose their hold regard the triumphs won by others as acts of imposture and charlatanism. The painter, whose art is one of deception, had usually to veil this theme of deception, of disillusionment, otherwise he would have incriminated himself. Sometimes, however, he would delicately suggest the deceit of his personages.

GIAMBATTISTA TIEPOLO (1696-1770). THE CHARLATAN, 1756. MUSEO DE BELLAS ARTES, BARCELONA.

ANTOINE WATTEAU (1684-1721). ITALIAN COMEDIANS, ABOUT 1720. NATIONAL GALLERY OF ART, WASHINGTON, D.C.
SAMUEL H. KRESS COLLECTION.

JEAN-FRANÇOIS DE TROY (1679-1752).
THE DECLARATION OF LOVE, 1731. GEMÄLDEGALERIE, STAATLICHE MUSEEN, BERLIN-DAHLEM.

ANTOINE WATTEAU (1684-1721). THE PILGRIMAGE TO CYTHERA, 1717. GEMÄLDEGALERIE, STAATLICHE MUSEEN, BERLIN-DAHLEM.

JEAN-HONORÉ FRAGONARD (1732-1806). THE FÊTE AT RAMBOUILLET, OR THE ISLE OF LOVE, ABOUT 1780. CALOUSTE GULBENKIAN FOUNDATION, LISBON.

FROM LIGHT FRIVOLITIES
TO MACABRE DELIGHTS

To paint for the joy of painting is to forget that one is painting for the pleasure of the wealthy. An unstable complicity united the whim of the patrons and the imagination of the artists. The patron believed he was making the decisions, yet he was following, through the particular fashions, the forms suggested by the painters: he made up his mind according to the works currently being admired. The painter, for his part, wished he could invent, but was too anxious to please to be able to invent in complete freedom. The artist who perceived this might well chafe. Between the imperatives of social success and the unhindered search for beauty, between the requirements of a specific commission and the soarings of inspiration, a compromise intervened, as best it could, and became a style. The painter's hand was free only within the limits accorded by the pleasure of his public. It is true that a libertine, free-thinking public was prepared to encourage freedom for artists; but they wanted this freedom to be exercised in a particular vein, that of the anecdote. The painter was therefore subjected to the *scene*, and was free only to treat it licentiously. (Whoever wished to avoid this servitude had to find refuge in still life, submitting himself to servile imitation of the object in order to regain freedom of technique.)

If the parvenu demanded insipid galant politeness, if he looked on the painter as one of the "ministers" to his pleasures, like any wig-maker, cook, or chorus-girl, if he supervised the composition and execution down to the shading of a hand or the opening of a tunic, it was for the painter to relive, in his own way, Hegel's relationship between master and slave: he was humiliated, regarded as a purveyor of pictures, as a mere artisan. At this time he was quite unable to rebel and assume his complete independence. His sole outlet, before he began to be supported by the written commentaries of authors and philosophers, was to forewarn public taste, molding it imperceptibly, to engage sympathy by

creations which followed the diffuse aspirations of the period, and perhaps even to initiate these aspirations and give them precise form. Simultaneously hemmed in and defiant, the painter could exercise his liberty only in so far as he could create figures capable of catching the attention of a public in search of unknown emotions, novelty, quick stimulation...

The various refinements of hedonism could then be paradoxical. They could mime spiritual flights of devotion, be sublimated to the point of an apparent renunciation of pleasure. The idea of a disinterested form of beauty was not without its attraction for those wearied of self-seeking beauty. *Amor non mercenarius*: a pleasure aimed solely at the harmony of forms; an art which, abandoning its role of providing a restless "edgy" public with the stimulants for good or bad sentiments, called for meditation, for the pure gaze of the soul. The sovereign pleasure would thus reside in observing the fulfillment of creative freedom according to the artist's own interior law.

This purity was little more than one temptation amongst several. When, as the century advanced, sensibilities became passionate, anxious, unruly, the artist, experiencing the same moral climate, answered the call and dedicated himself to the drama. Here he discovered a possible application for his idle energies.

At the time when, in the words of Sénac de Meilhan, the "sexagenarian spirit of the century" was becoming widespread, the art lover was seeking to enliven his pleasures by pursuing unusual or perverse experiences. For boredom follows hard on pleasure—this was one of the favorite themes of the period. The same sensations, too often repeated, no longer surprise. The attractions of geographical exoticism pall rapidly. But there remained a further resource: the exoticism of evil. It remained for men to penetrate the dark continent of terror and forbidden pleasures, "to convert pain into sensual delight." This formula could have been taken from the Marquis de Sade: it is from Jean-Jacques Rousseau. Again, a certain intoxication with exalted virtue was equally attractive; it was a new exoticism, the tearful uprooting and removal of beneficence. It mattered little, according to Diderot, that passion should be carried to the limits of good or to the excesses of evil, provided that it contained greatness, provided that an expansive energy was offered for admiration. Don Juan puts his hand into that of the statue. Fidelio will face death to save Florestan. At the end of the century, around the time of the revolutionary crisis, pleasure was no longer to be found in easy, inconsequential adventures, but in a display of rebellious willpower, braving destiny or divine authority.

This was one of the strongest convictions of the *Sturm und Drang*; and it was one of the predominant themes in the art of Goya and Fuseli. One need simply observe, in their works of imagination, the metamorphosis which transforms the female face. Woman—persecutor or persecuted, murderess or tortured victim, desecrating or desecrated—woman is no longer the queen who ruled in the Rococo boudoirs. The beautiful "object" is the instrument (active or passive) of a grotesque black pleasure. Whether they inflict it or suffer it, a work of destruction is performed, in which the reverse of pleasure is no longer simply boredom, but death. Brought thus to the level of tragedy, the ephemeral resplendency of acute pleasure took on the appearance of bloody sacrifice and assumed a sacred dimension. Archaic phantasms appeared, and atheistic free-thinking reinvented the darker forms of belief, attracted towards funereal sights for the sake of the chilling shudder. In England some of the best-bred gentlemen—George Selwyn, Thomas Warton—are held to have reveled in executions. Edmund Burke considered that such spectacles could give rise to a sentiment different from pleasure, a more powerful emotion which he calls "delight." Let us suppose, says Burke, that a theater presents the finest tragedy imaginable—the death portrayed is none the less fictitious; if they announce that an important criminal is to be executed in the neighboring square, the theater will empty in a trice. "The passions which turn on self-preservation, turn on pain and danger; they are delightful when we have an idea of pain and danger without being

actually in such circumstances; this delight I have not called pleasure, because it turns on pain, and because it is different enough from any idea of positive pleasure. Whatever excites this delight, I call *sublime*." The sublimity of the sight of bloodletting comes from the fact that it is considered purely as a spectacle. In so far as our own life and the lives of our near relations are not threatened, we should experience before London in ruins the shudder of the sublime. "We seem here to have the reality regarded as a representation, i.e. in abstraction from its real bearing and interest; for, as Burke insists, no normal person *wishes* for such a real catastrophe as he will run to see where it takes place. So that, by a reverse movement compared with that of Plato, by elevating reality to the rank of an aesthetic semblance, instead of lowering art to the rank of useful reality, we seem to have started the suggestion that reality can be looked at aesthetically if looked at without practical interest, and therefore that the aesthetic temper consists, in part at least, in the absence of such interest" (Bosanquet). The tendency described here is not simply of theoretical importance. The elevation of reality to the level of aesthetic appearance anticipates the whole program of dandyism, and it is no surprise that this attitude, as also the corresponding theory, was born in the aristocratic circles of eighteenth-century England.

In the context of idle leisure, boredom, surfeited blasé amateurism, men began to treat objects and beings as part of the arbitrary phantasmagoria of their desires, unburdening them of their weight of reality. Staged appropriately, the whole of life could be transposed to an imaginary plane and become a work of art. Given this outlook, the pleasures of others, their sufferings, even their deaths, all became mere elements of a representation which a privileged consciousness might offer itself for the pleasure of a solitary, narcissistic self-indulgence. In the extreme examples of this attitude, with Sade or Beckford, it is evident that their minds had returned to the infantile stage at which a person is incapable of discerning any difference between his own phantasms and the existence of other people. Macabre "black pleasure," in the form which it took throughout the century (with the help of whips, cantharides, etc.), was the extreme manifestation of the whim of the solipsist who, raising life to the level of art, treats good and evil, suffering and self-indulgence, as just so much material for aesthetic creations. Anxiety is hidden beneath the illusion of omnipotence, parodying the powers of some god who conjures up an imaginary world and punishes it as the desire takes him. The aestheticizing vision of reality replaces objects by their appearance, and allows the individual to withdraw into the infantile illusion of the magical supremacy of its own desires; by the same token, horror, torture, destruction become mere spectacles, tableaux offered purely for the onlooker's pleasure (or, according to Burke, for his "delight"). This imaginary dramatization soon developed towards satanism: the isolated individual, imprisoned in his own dream and incapable of reaching reality, tried to gain stature by assuming a dramatic pose of defiance against God, and to prove it to himself he accumulated the most heinous crimes, which he either lived in his imagination or invented from life. The violent thrust of energy which characterized the second half of the century found an outlet in this direction, involving certain lives in a vicious, dissolute fiction, or else in the secondary fiction of the fanciful, romantic representation of a life dedicated to the imaginary.

Was this the growth and spread of a *violent* form of freedom? In the event, the imaginative outbursts of this embryonic romanticism seem to be less a manifestation of true liberty than the sign of a certain fearfulness in entering upon new adult responsibilities. For Kant, the sense of the *Aufklärung* was the coming-of-age, the emancipation of the intellect which could now dare to evade the yoke of traditional authority and think independently. As regards the exponents of macabre pleasure, it would not be merely speaking figuratively to say that they took fright when facing emancipation. Rather than uphold the onerous liberty which maintains that all things must be referred back to a hidden internal law, they preferred to blaspheme against the traditional figure of the Father. They retired into a dreamworld of defiance and culpability, in order to incur an eventual punishment which would prove the reality of a Presence they could not dispense with.

Between the sumptuous profusions of the Rococo and the attitude we have just described there is a recognizable continuity. The tendency of luxury, with its proliferation of minute adornments, is so to saturate the trappings of life that life itself is literally absorbed into its surrounding splendor.

From shoe-buckles to garden designs, from table forks to pieces of ordnance, besides a continuity of style, there is, within this style and through the ornamental design, the desire to avoid any break in succession, any interstice breaking up the artistic continuity: if decorative artifice abhors the void to this extent and tends irresistibly to occupy the space available, it is in order to constitute a self-contained world in which life can be lived as a representation. What might originally have been nothing but a sign of the possession of wealth, becomes a form of magic through which life is transposed to a different dimension and, in the pursuit of pleasure, tends toward unreality.

Here the theatrical role of the façade takes on its full significance. Facing the outside world, on the side opposite the prompter, the façade marks the limit of a privileged universe, with an elegant display of signs imposing *an illusion of authority*. Within, on the prompt-side or behind closed doors, there are for those who live in this domain the mirrors and wainscoting which establish, conversely, *the authority of illusion*.

From the fairy tale to the Gothic novel, from Boucher's nymphs to Fuseli's tortured sleepers—where did the transformation take place? Fiction had always dominated, and it did so now more than ever: but now it could dispense with finery, easy charms, silks and stylish furnishings. The imagination now despised the fine products of luxury handicrafts, aware that it could develop its own medium, organizing the scene as it saw fit, without seeking the complicity of tailors, hairdressers or tapestry-makers. The life of the imagination was no longer dazzled by innumerable delicacies of background, it no longer sought its stimulants outside itself, in the false artifice of others. The imagination took its inspiration from its own independent power; it invented and created—and it discovered that its flight contained a certain excess and disproportion which imparted an even greater enjoyment. No doubt this spread of the imagination into the fantastic implied the most lively derision for the gilded cages in which it had previously allowed itself to be imprisoned. The creative dream now recognized no other frontiers than those which it imposed upon itself: death, night, the abyss. But in escaping from the trifling constraints of the pretty, it was casting aside a frivolous décor only to set up in its place another, artificial, purely imaginary and excessive décor—it was repudiating the artificial social masque only to introduce an illusory dramaturgy of ghosts. The gloomy castles invented by Sade differ from the country houses of wealthy society: they have the total unreality of the dream, as opposed to the semi-unreality of the social comedy. They consist entirely of *representation* (in both the theatrical and the psychological sense of the term), they are solely the projection of an isolated desire, eternally unattainable; whereas *salon* life is a perpetual compromise between the real and the unreal. Fiction as a whole became more fiery, and more hostile towards the minor forms of the imaginary. In its frenzy the imagination laid claim to a truth in the name of which it condemned all futile inventions. And yet it was itself nothing more than a fanatical invention, and its energies recoiled in part against itself. The mortal fury which inspired and animated the imagination, and seemed determined to lay bare even the ultimate mysteries of human life, could equally well be directed against the very illusion that nourished these flights of the imagination. Thus the scenes of destruction so frequent in Fuseli and Goya could be seen to indicate a latent self-destruction, to imply a search for some way of escape from the unreality which marked the evolution of their art. Fuseli remained a prisoner of his scenography. But Goya, fascinated by the monsters brought forth by his rationalized dreams, does seem to have succeeded, once at least, in escaping from the dream. It seems as though the dream of gallantry or foppishness had first to develop into nightmare, and that in this nightmare the artist had to struggle wildly, at the extreme limits of agony, until he emerged into a barren land, beyond the imaginary, beyond images. He then painted an empty sky.

FROM THE SWING TO THE SCAFFOLD

The painter catches and records a fleeting instant. The Rococo artist sought to lend that pictorial moment a special eloquence, to suggest the particular significance of the transient situation, in short to represent an occasion. The pleasure it gives arises not so much from conscious calculation as from a fortuitous combination of circumstances. It is the large part played by chance and sensual appeal that distinguishes the scènes galantes *of the Rococo from the dramatic pathos of the "grand style" and of history painting, both of which were inherited from the Baroque.*

In the two pictures by Fragonard, we have quick glimpses of the thrill of expectation kindled by a sudden contact with, or the sight of, a female body poised between surrender and retreat or flight. With an obscure accomplice in the background, the girl is about to swing back again. The other glimpse shows a daughter, caught up by her stealthy lover, but already glancing towards the half-open door, behind which sits a vigilant mother. Who knows whether such moments will ever come again?

Woman was not always so gently enticed, such a gentle, willing prey. The eighteenth century had not forgotten the darker eroticism of the Baroque age, which saw in woman an object of torment or a harbinger of death. About the time of the Neoclassical revival, certain artists began to treat this theme differently: they replaced representations of premeditated violence by evocations of the intermediate stages of consciousness, cataleptic states, and semblances of death. These recumbent bodies are sometimes actually dead, and, as in the legend that clings to Young (the author of Night Thoughts*), their haunting fascination lies in the suggestion of necrophilia and incest.*

Fuseli's sleeping woman is stretched out at full length, in an attitude of surrender that conceals nothing of the ecstasy experienced beyond her anguish and convulsions. But the line of the horizontal body in its utter abandon develops into a vertical fall. She is the victim of some supernatural force. We sense dizzily that she is going to fall, that she is actually falling, her reeling world oppressed by the weight of the nightmare demon.

ANTOINE WATTEAU (1684-1721). THE SERENADER. MUSÉE CONDÉ, CHANTILLY.

JEAN-HONORÉ FRAGONARD (1732-1806). THE SWING, 1766. PRIVATE COLLECTION.

JEAN-HONORÉ FRAGONARD (1732-1806). THE STOLEN KISS, ABOUT 1766. HERMITAGE, LENINGRAD.

GIOVANNI BATTISTA PIAZZETTA (1682-1754). JUDITH AND HOLOFERNES. GALLERIA CORSINI, ROME.

GIAMBATTISTA TIEPOLO (1696-1770). THE BEHEADING OF JOHN THE BAPTIST, 1733. NATIONALMUSEUM, STOCKHOLM.

HENRY FUSELI (1741-1825). THE NIGHTMARE. FROM THE COLLECTION OF THE DETROIT INSTITUTE OF ARTS.

III

ANXIETY AND FESTIVITY

REVELRY AND ITS AFTERMATH

From the revels of the *fêtes galantes* to the revelry of the French Revolution the internal transformations of the century can be seen in the changes which took place in the manifold ceremonial of pleasure.

We ought by rights to seek out the original sources, or, at the very least, go back to the festivals of the Renaissance and the Baroque. Around the princes, in the courts, these festivities offered the opportunity for a magical transmutation of reality. All the arts combined, under the wand of an all-powerful enchanter, to transform space, halt time, and display, sometimes for several days on end, the agreeable consequences of a fable created by the great and their followers. What was left, by the beginning of the eighteenth century, of those regulated, composite festivities, in which courtiers would make their entrance in carefully studied figures, striving after a perfect combination of music and dance? Very little. Princely festivities now appeared rarely to be solemn, spectacular, illusionary ceremonies. They were no longer governed by any internal ordinance; the participants had no longer to become actors in a preconceived set game. Balls, dinners, spectacles brought them together in disorder, increasing the gaiety of the surroundings by innumerable objects of delectation. Although masks, disguises, anonymity still played their part, the essential aim was no longer to play, but to steal by unseen, to watch secretly—and yet to be recognized through the disguise. The disguises were not roles to be maintained but adornments, instruments of seduction, of access and flight. In the life of a social group dedicated to the pursuit of pleasure, festivities, with their expense and artful contrivances, seemed to be moments of truth, when individuals could indulge their predominant passions singlemindedly and almost completely unhindered. This was expenditure *par excellence* in a life devoted to expenditure. But it was also *par excellence* the isolated instant of time in a life composed of an anxious series of instants. Festivities brought together, for a brief lapse of time, a very close succession of instants, of almost continuous pleasures, so that the enraptured mind was incessantly occupied. This continuously renewed Present was all-embracing, monopolizing the attention of these fickle beings who always gave priority to immediate, present objects. Festivities brought about this "rapid continuity of pleasure" (La Morlière, *Angola*) by innumerable meetings of persons and random encounters. Quickly exhausted and wearied, men urgently sought out other instants, new objects— and found them. They wanted to repeat the experience by diversity—so they diversified. For these festivities organized a maximum of variety, a perpetual triumph of surprise, an ostentatious semblance of eternal energy (together with an underlying premonition of impending weariness, of heavy boredom).

It is only to be expected that such festivities, with their essential plurality, should tend towards disintegration. With Watteau, this disintegration can be sensed in the very structure of his compositions. His gatherings are caught in a state of instability. In both time and space we stand at the fringe of the festivity, just as it is about to begin, or as it is fading away: when the actors are making their opening bow, or when the pilgrimage to Cythera is ending: in expectancy or in reminiscence of the pleasure. The characters, delighted and delighting, are always just skirting the pleasure. But such intervals are unavoidable. This is the essential law of pleasure: for "permanent pleasure is not pleasure" (Voltaire). The revelry must afterwards be renewed, reinvented in other forms. Debauchery and outdoor parties: heavy, insensate revelry. Hunting and war: festivals of ritual. Dinners: festivals of gluttony. Gaming: an abstract revelry in which the anxieties of chance absorb and distract one's whole being. Concerts, operas... and all the petty give and take of manifold ceremonial which perpetuates the spirit of festivity. The luxury of everyday furnishings, the mountainous chandeliers of crystal: these are a frozen, motionless festivity, revelry solidified. And the preludes to festivity! Elegant outings in carriages are festivities in miniature with their sumptuousness and their hazards.

Boredom is always close. Dissipation, which Madame Du Deffand considers the remedy for boredom, is only a palliative, containing its own judgment: the mind wastes itself away in its effort to escape. The fireworks fall back to earth. Day must sooner or later dawn; and in the hard light of day, after the weariness of pleasure, the faces which had seemed so alluring by candlelight show the ravages of their excesses. Such is the strange surprise, according to Steele, awaiting the husband of a heavily made-up woman: "Their skin is so tarnished with this practice that when she first wakes in the morning, she scarce seems young enough to be the mother of her whom I carried to bed the night before." In retrospect, the enchantment of the revelry is nothing more than a delusion. Behind the discontinuous succession of instants during which the vain surprises of renewal had been repeated seemingly endlessly, a different time was secretly at work— the destructive time which carries all things towards death. La Morlière's *Angola* describes the varied misunderstandings of lovers and, as Robert Mauzi has shown, all leads up to a moment of macabre disenchantment and inevitable disgrace: "The ball was almost over, the candles were burning low; the players, drunk or fast asleep, had abandoned their instruments; the crowd had thinned and everyone had let fall their masks; *huge streams* of red and white *paint* flowed down these faces, revealing *livid flesh, blotched and flabby*—a disgusting spectacle of decayed coquetry." Here we recognize one of the favorite themes of the Baroque mind: disillusionment *(el desengaño)* before a reality which seems to sneer all the more for having been so seductive in its illusory adornments. In the seventeenth century, the somber or grotesque discoveries brought by disillusionment led to a spiritual conversion, offering a choice between the ephemeral and the eternal, between the vanity of the world and the firm truths of the faith. In the eighteenth century, the arts and literature, traditional accomplices of illusion, rarely expressed this tendency towards conversion. When Hogarth or Goya evoke the decrepitude of aging coquettes, the disillusion that they illustrate is not entirely free of moral aims,

but the satire is heavy with despair. For there is nothing to invite us to go beyond the disillusionment: in recognizing the grotesque ravages wrought upon the painted flesh, they are revealing a reality which seems to lack either future possibilities or any compensatory opposite. The disillusionment is not just one stage of a spiritual itinerary, it is a final judgment. Revelry had been necessary to snatch these anxious minds and bodies from their torpor; and after the revels they simply remained dazed and blank.

Thus nighttime, which the "aristocratic" merrymaking seemingly wished to annihilate with its thousand-and-one flickering lights, takes its revenge. I do not, however, wish to link this image of "aristocratic" revelry to the nobility alone. I use the term primarily to cover a determination to reserve admission to the revelry to a group privileged by birth and wealth. The company came together by virtue of a given *distinction* which separated them from the rest of mankind. They gathered together, taking care to establish a certain distance, to maintain a divergence. Further, within the group itself, each participant, intent on his own pleasure, isolated himself yet again. The insistence with which each individual concentrated upon savoring the propitious moment cut him off in the midst of the crowd; and the revelry around him was simply a living picture of the pleasures he could himself lay claim to. Through this type of festivity runs the paradox of a gathering of individuals whose egocentric desires lend themselves exquisitely to the dissociation of their individual experiences. Just as these instants of pleasure had neither past nor future, so these individuals seemed to wish neither to share nor to communicate. Their pleasure was consumed as it came; it celebrated nothing beyond itself and the blinding light of its own brief passage.

They invited the intellect (by which we mean the artist, the poet) into their festivities, for the intellect could decorate and animate their pleasure. But by this they were inviting closer inspection, a watchfulness that was awake to the empty scene of the early morning. A new criticism, no longer hoodwinked, was to arise, longing for a type of festival which might found something durable: civic friendship, love for the prince, a union of hearts. There arose a desire for a festival, a feast, in the broadest sense of the term, which would no longer be "exclusive" (Rousseau) but would include and unite a whole people, break down social barriers, group together classes which had been separated. This would involve nothing less than an inversion of the internal energy of the aristocratic festival, introducing the mutual consideration and intercommunication that the privileged groups had spurned, mingling the conditions that they had kept separate. Admittedly, the *ancien régime* did organize lavish public festivals, for such events as births, marriages or peace treaties. They would arrange theatrical settings in the streets for a few hours, designed by the best architects: triumphal arches, allegorical figures, fountains flowing with wine. The populace was invited to watch the procession of guards, officers, princes, with a finale of illuminations and fireworks. These moving, ephemeral works of art, have been recorded for us in a few revealing engravings.

Festivals for the populace—but did this make them *popular* festivals? The people thronged to them, were even suffocated in the crush. But if they were trampled down at the Corpus Christi procession this was hardly attributable to any outburst of faith: Sébastien Mercier claims that they came out of idle curiosity. "They admired the progress and order of the procession, the canopy, the monstrance, the regular swing of the thuribles, the beauty of the ornaments: they heard the military music, interspersed with frequent, majestic discharges..." The people did not participate deeply in the celebrations they were invited to. In 1780, Mercier declared that the people of Paris had lost their gaiety. So the authorities intervened to give more warmth to the manifestation: "The police take care, in certain circumstances, to hire good lusty shouters who go off into different quarters of the town to stir the others up, as for instance with the rowdy, masked *chianlis* during the pre-Lenten festival. But true manifestations of public joy, as of popular contentment, are such that they cannot be imitated." In one contemporary event, however, Mercier's *Tableau de Paris* discovers a genuine celebration, and the circumstances are revealing: the common people, on the Feast of St Louis, are invited inside the Tuileries and the royal gardens; then, for a few hours, the barriers that divide social classes are abandoned. "This huge social gathering offers a most singular, most animated picture, particularly in moonlight: all levels of society mingle indiscriminately, varying the spectacle and enlivening it—a picturesque and curious sight. I must say that this is the one day of the year when I like the Tuileries to any degree..." Sébastien Mercier, an anticlerical freemason, was not alone in this opinion, this aspiration: it was a desire for a solemn *collective* occasion incorporating at once a celebration and a form of worship. Disapproving equally the orgies of the rich and the ceremonies of the Church, he seems to have desired that the joy of a whole assembled people should be a kind of synthesis of a pleasure party and a religious act.

ANTOINE WATTEAU (1684-1721). GILLES, ABOUT 1718 (?). LOUVRE, PARIS.

GILLES

"Watteau," we read in the Encyclopédie, *"was misanthropic and given to melancholy; yet his pictures, as a rule, represent only cheerful and entertaining scenes. This taste, so much at variance with his character, may have come from the habit he had in his youth of watching the 'act' put on by mountebanks in order to collect a crowd, and sketching them directly from life." But is the contrast really so great in this picture? Gilles, a stock character of the Théâtre de la Foire, gave Watteau an opportunity of confessing his own melancholy in the figure of an actor held up to ridicule. Unlike the mountebanks who dazzle the crowd with their patter, Gilles is the image of taciturn naiveness and conscious failure.* A laver la tête d'un âne l'on perd sa lessive *—such is the title of the play in which he has the leading part, and the sad-looking animal with the Doctor astride it brings home the point of the allegory.*

Standing motionless, his arms dangling at his side, clad in satin as spotless as his mind is blank, the figure of Gilles suggests that of a bemused man, caught between sleeping and waking, his mind paralyzed in a tangle of confusion. This stupor, this lethargy, was experienced and described by the sharpest minds of the century: it was the necessary antithesis of the extreme wit and intelligence of such lively figures as Harlequin and Figaro.

Dora Panofsky has pointed out that this frontal pose corresponds closely to that of the Gilles (or Pierrot) in the center of the Italian Comedians; *furthermore, the composition of this picture, showing the actors taking their bow at the end of the performance, is strikingly similar to that of Rembrandt's* Ecce Homo, *which Watteau so much admired. Thus, by an interplay of allusion, parody and transposition, the comic mystery of human stupidity is merged with the sacred mystery of defiled innocence:* sancta simplicitas.

THE REIGN OF THE MASK

Venice at Carnival time was marked by a frenzied delectation in freedom. "Wearing a mask, you can dare anything and say anything; the Republic sanctions and protects the wearing of masks. With a mask on, you may go where you will, to salons, divine services, convents, balls, to the Ducal Palace, to the Ridotto... A strip of white satin over your face, and on your shoulders a hood of black lace or taffeta, reaching down to the flowing folds of the mantle, and by means of this ridiculous disguise, aristocratic Venice becomes democratic... But the mask is more than a disguise, it is an incognito. It is secrecy, anonymity, confident impunity, it is licensed folly and licit nonsense... You can recognize no one, and no one recognizes you. You cannot tell who has just accosted you with such strange remarks, who has elbowed you sharply, who is beckoning you furtively, shadowing you through the maze of narrow streets, sitting down with you now for coffee; you do not know whose white and timid slipper is tremblingly pressing your shoe" (Philippe Monnier).

Only a civilization enamored of shows and pageantry, a civilization stressing primarily the pleasures of the eye, could cultivate this art of disguise and masquerade. The masked Carnival afforded everyone the pleasure of seeing and being seen without revealing his own identity; they revealed only an arbitrary aspect of themselves, which they could vary with time and place as the fancy took them. Released from all the entangling circumstances of class and profession, the person behind the mask was no more than the particular image he chose to flaunt, his whole being was temporarily contained in the words he happened to make up on the spur of the moment. Like an actor, a masked man exists entirely in the present: his freedom is unbounded, and is protected by the recognition that he is only acting, arbitrarily and deceitfully.

Thus the actress, admired by the whole audience, captivates and charms them because she is disguised in another personality, casting through the fugitive inflections of her voice a spell impervious to the light of truth.

PIETRO LONGHI (1702-1785). THE SOIRÉE, ABOUT 1757. PINACOTECA QUERINI-STAMPALIA, VENICE.

FRANCESCO GUARDI (1712-1793). THE GALA CONCERT, 1782. BAYERISCHE STAATSGEMÄLDESAMMLUNGEN, MUNICH.

FRANÇOIS DE CUVILLIÈS THE ELDER (1695-1768). INTERIOR OF THE OLD RESIDENCY THEATER, MUNICH, 1751-1753.

LUIS PARET (1746-1799). MASKED BALL, 1766. PRADO, MADRID.

ENTERTAINMENT AND SATIRE

The theater-going public expected each act of an opera to include an entertainment—its troupe of dancers, its show within the show. In the buoyant world of the opera, the ballet introduced a further degree of lightness—levity within levity. The pirouettes of Camargo and Vestris expressed the quintessence of carefree agility, the abolition of the constraints of gravity.

The same public liked paintings to record fashionable entertainments or dances, incorporating the actual setting (parks, theaters and pavilions) and including a faithful portrayal of the participants. But these real entertainments were practically indistinguishable from the wholly imaginary, ideal gatherings in which painters conjured up a vision of the "charms of life." In these paintings, happiness was represented as a display of energy entirely devoted to perfecting the grace of each separate gesture and movement. Happiness was to be found in activity for activity's sake, and in repose or relaxation without quiescence: dancing was the perfect embodiment of this ideal of leisured movement.

Watteau's followers seldom depart from a stereotyped image of these entertainments, as if no one could ever tire of these minuets under eternal blue skies, far from the great historical movements of the century and the commonplace obligations of everyday life. But it was an illusory image, like that of the gardens of Armida or the golden age. The century pretended to revel in these scenes—but its participation was superficial. It was easy for the satirists to show up this discrepancy. They made it plain that men lived otherwise, that real life was often foolish, dull and vulgar. Hogarth was a past master in the art of exposing man's follies and foibles. For the couple in Marriage à la Mode, *the life of pleasure leads to melodramatic adultery, crime, and death. But even this scene is only a prelude to the drama; in the early hours, husband and wife have each returned from a different party, weary and befuddled. The steward who has come to present the bills turns away in disgust, lifting his eyes to heaven. The liabilities are mounting.*

JEAN-BAPTISTE PATER (1695-1736). THE FAIR AT BEZONS, ABOUT 1733. THE METROPOLITAN MUSEUM OF ART, NEW YORK. THE JULES S. BACHE COLLECTION, 1949.

MICHEL BARTHÉLEMY OLIVIER (1712-1784). THE FÊTE AT L'ISLE-ADAM, 1766. MUSÉE DU CHÂTEAU, VERSAILLES.

NICOLAS LANCRET (1690-1743). DANCE IN A PAVILION, ABOUT 1720. SCHLOSS CHARLOTTENBURG, BERLIN.

WILLIAM HOGARTH (1697-1764). MARRIAGE À LA MODE, II: BREAKFAST. UNDATED.
REPRODUCED BY COURTESY OF THE TRUSTEES, THE NATIONAL GALLERY, LONDON.

THE FESTIVAL OF ICONOCLASM

This new aspect of the festival, at first entirely imaginary, which originally appeared in the musings of idealistic writers, in a few ardent pages by Diderot and Rousseau, was to inspire a whole generation. For art, this "theory of the festival" played a dual role. On the one hand, it was in the name of this unanimous enthusiasm that they condemned the forms, works, music, the whole décor associated with the tradition of the aristocratic festivals, exclusive and scattered. As a result, the popular festival, wishing to introduce pure spontaneity, began in an ecstasy of iconoclasm. On the other hand, although this new conception of the festival aspired towards simplicity and frugality, it was very quickly to prompt the appearance of new decorative forms: in its efforts to meet the needs of reality, it was itself to adopt ceremonial and costumes, erect monuments.

The controversy was launched in connection with the theater. Think of the admirable auditoriums of the eighteenth-century theaters still in existence: in Munich, Venice, Versailles. It is clear that such theaters could have been considered by the eighteenth century as the supreme expression of a civilization intoxicated with luxury and pleasure. Compared ironically to temples (as the actresses were compared to vestals), the theaters were at once the sacred domain of elegant frivolity and the places where literary and musical exaltation could reach its climax.

Philosophers, aspiring after truth, were to contrast the ideal function of the spectacle with its present reality. The theater might have been an act of communion, but for each of the smartly dressed theatergoers parading up and down it was simply an opportunity for displaying some personal distinction, a pretext for private enjoyment. The theater was missing its true mark: it ought to have been a place where human solidarity could be affirmed, where the high truth of a communal presence could be made manifest. Instead of being a genuine home of human integrity, it was a palace of deceiving appearances.

A singular stroke of evil introduced separation in all domains: the very precincts of the theater, rather than imposing unity upon those within, marked a frontier excluding those without. As for the audience itself, they had no unity whatsoever: an infinite distance separated the turbulent pit from the inattentive boxes. Rousseau, in his *Lettre sur les spectacles,* denounced in the strongest terms this division of beings, the estranged, private pleasure which each person sought for himself, in which the repressive forces of egotism checked any expansive movements of sympathy. "Under the illusion of gathering together for the spectacle, each person actually isolates himself: they go there to forget about their relatives, friends, neighbors..." Improving on the same idea, Sébastien Mercier attacked one of the special characteristics of contemporary theater design: the multiplication of *small boxes*, little cells of private life juxtaposed as in a bee-hive; in each box there reigned in splendor a tyrannical queen, who had come to the spectacle with the sole aim of being wooed by suitors; the opening facing the stage was less important than the door to the corridor, the entrance for chattering friends and flatterers: "If you are a woman, you must have your spaniel, your cushion, your footwarmer; but above all else some little foppish dolt with opera glasses who will describe all the comings and goings and name all the actors. At the same time, in the lady's fan there is a space in which a piece of glass is mounted, so that she can see without being seen... The public stands outside the theater, money in hand, because some boxes are reserved for the whole year, and—often enough—stand empty." In contrast to this piecemeal gathering, which is divided up by private personal whims, Rousseau and Diderot describe nostalgically the festival gatherings of the ancients or the improvisations of popular festivals, in which they saw the fullness of collective joy. The Greek theater had transformed the crowd of spectators into a single homogeneous being. "How fine humanity is at the spectacle! Why should they separate so quickly! Men are so good, so happy, when courtesy unites their separate wills, merges them, makes them one!" But what was to be done? Simply create a new theater? Or dream of going away with a few friends to found a colony on the isle of Lampedusa? Diderot was quite aware that you cannot change the nature of festival gatherings without altering the structure of society. Rousseau, who preferred Lacedaemon instead, also wished that public ceremonies could grip the onlookers to the point of binding them in a sense of unity: "We should not adopt those exclusive spectacles which enclose a small number of people in the sadness of some obscure retreat, which hold them fearful and motionless in silence and inaction, which offer them nothing beyond the sight of partitions, iron points, soldiers, distressing images of servitude and inequality. No, these are no festivals for such as you, oh happy peoples. It is in the open air, under the skies, that you must gather together to enjoy the sweetness of your happiness... Let the sunlight shine down on your innocent spectacle. You will be yourselves a spectacle—and the sun could not shine on a worthier sight.

"But what shall be the objects of the spectacle? What shall be shown? Nothing, if you so wish. Wherever there is liberty and public concourse, there too will be well-being. Set up a pole, crowned with flowers, in the middle of the public square, have the people assemble—and you will have a festival. Better still, let the spectators partake in the spectacle, make them actors themselves, let each person see himself and love himself *in* the others, and they will be the more closely united."

The festival that Rousseau envisaged was therefore an assembly of people aware that their own presence was the basis of their fervor: they could look at one another with a joyful sense of their shared freedom. Each person being equal to the rest, their awareness of this reciprocity would be the very substance of the gathering. They would celebrate a new transparency: hearts would hide no more secrets, communication would be completely free of obstacles. Since everyone present would be simultaneously audience and actors, they would have done away with the distance which, in the theater, separated the stage and the auditorium. The spectacle would be everywhere and nowhere. Identical in everyone's eyes, the image of the festival would be indivisible—and it would be the image, multiplied indefinitely, of man meeting man in absolute equality and understanding. The festival would be marked less by any wealth of background ornamentation than by a significant abolition of all such decoration. In this way the physical space would itself be free to receive the all-pervading joy. All outside images should disappear. "What shall be shown? Nothing, if you so wish." This abolition of representations could not be overemphasized. When the festival is present in men's hearts, theaters are redundant. Why have recourse to illusions when there is a superabundance of truth poised ready to dominate the gathering through and through? This power which rejected the use of images (because it recognized only its own image) was quickly to instigate iconoclastic ventures. The system of façades, screens, fictions, alluring masks which dominated the world of aristocratic culture could no longer be retained: they were condemned to disappear, for they were felt in future to be simply inert elements, harmful obstacles. The iconoclastic abolition of decorative background proclaimed that collective presence in itself, by its own intensity, sufficed to create the universal impact of the festival. Compared with the elaborate, decorative festival, the "frugal festival" took advantage of a great increase in expansive energy: it could arouse spontaneously all the splendor and all the solemnity that the other only achieved by means of the arts of illusion. Every ornament rejected would suppress an impure influence that could catch the attention and prevent the people from being united in a spirit of mutual confidence. Private covetous desires could no longer be kept simmering spitefully: one's desires, in virtuous sublimation, would be directed towards a unity of minds. At its most intense heat, the general joy would reabsorb all individual appetites into itself. This community of wills would be sufficiently satisfying to cause the individual to renounce any other object of desire. There would be, literally, no more objects. For this regenerated festival would be nothing other than the awakening of a collective subject, born to itself, becoming aware of itself in all its members, in each of its participants.

In the name of transparency of hearts, a demanding form of austerity made a completely clean sweep of all images, and established a cult of pure presence. Others besides Rousseau shared this aspiration. All the great community movements of the period advanced in the same direction, whether they were religious, like Pietism and Methodism, or political, like Jacobinism towards the end of the century, imbued with the ideas of Rousseau. Eventually the demolitions effected by the Revolution were to take on an air of festivity, and the revolutionary festivals were to cast into the flames all the symbols of the *ancien régime*. When the king's head fell, the guillotine was destroying, spectacularly, a great *image*. National ceremonies in the open air were to be an attempt to organize visible mass movements in which the people could come face to face with itself, perceive itself.

Let us turn to another result of the same principle: on the level of fashions in dress, sansculottism is a revealing symptom. By this "popular" transformation of his appearance, the patriot was manifesting symbolically his rejection of self-important outward show, repudiating publicly all the sartorial attractions particular to the *ancien régime*—fashions which had given the body an aesthetic function. Breeches (*la culotte*), jackets, coats caught in at the waist, wigs, all enveloped the body in such a way as to reveal it, to show it off to advantage, to catch the eye with its attractive silks. Sansculottism was a vestimentary sign which minimized the flattering function of such dress. What mattered was no longer to please, but—as Coyer demanded as early as 1755—to "think communally"; so any effort to achieve elegance would be an implicit disaffection. Any man too well-dressed was instantly suspect: he was thinking of himself before thinking of the good of the people... The profound sense of the Thermidorian reaction lay in its lavish excess of coquetry. Royalist dandies, ultra-fashionable beaux and belles, caricaturing the *ancien régime's* concern with clothes, indicated that the Revolution had been brought to a halt.

From the theme of liberty there arose the fervent, intoxicating notion of banishing the prestige of the *spectacle*. Does this imply that the closing years of the century were turning away from an art of *representation*, were turning their interests towards other realities than those of the visible universe? This tendency is clear: it is no accident that, with the exception of artists like Goya, David or Ledoux, the greatest works of the late eighteenth century were symphonies or poems. The aim of this iconoclasm was to oppose a restricted form of art, paralyzed by its own visual and spatial materiality, a symbol of private wealth rather than of communicated feelings. Free and spontaneous, this fervor could not remain unexpressed: it invented new forms. It called for new means of expression which would catch its subjective out-

bursts without solidifying them into "external" figures, into a rigid theatrical décor: a music from the heart, with lights and shades which would create a genuine language of the passions; a non-descriptive form of poetry, freed from the subjection to visual images that a misunderstood tradition had imposed on it. Lessing's *Laocoon* formally opposed the old adage *ut pictura poesis*, in order to attribute to poetry a dramatic expression independent of all pictorial representation. This was a very clear definition of an art of interiority. For Hegel, romantic art was essentially musical and lyrical. But lyricism and music are to be experienced in a state of recollection; if they invite social communion it is on condition that the gathering should first of all fall silent. Romanticism speaks of communion to isolated individuals. What therefore is the solution for those who wish to introduce a new political order and celebrate it with festivals?

"Ah! What a fine festival we have celebrated this last week or so!... In place of the altar—or rather, of the charlatan stage—we had set up the throne of Liberty. Instead of a dead statue, we set upon it a living image of the divinity, a masterpiece of nature. A delightful woman, as beautiful as the goddess she represented, was seated at the top of a mountain, a revolutionary cap on her head, holding a pike in her hand, surrounded by all the pretty excommunicated Opera girls who, in their turn, damned the cloth with their more than angelic singing of patriotic hymns." Such is the free description which Hébert —*le Père Duchesne*—applies to the *Fête de la Raison*, celebrated in Notre-Dame on the 20th Brumaire in the year II (10th November 1793). The image is farcical, and the farce corresponds to a profound contradiction. The intention of the festival was not simply anti-Christian: this deliberate sacrilege of traditional religion took the form of a new consecration, a form of worship for the new community. Nothing, no doubt, was more sincere than this desire to replace the dead images by a living being, by the tangible stuff of life. Citizen Chaumette, haranguing the Convention, affirmed naively that iconoclasm was attacking simulacra in order to bring about the accession of real *presence*. "We have not offered our sacrifices to vain images, to inanimate idols. No: it is a masterpiece of nature that we have chosen to represent Reason; and our sacred image has inflamed every heart." Only, far from creating real presence, they fell into the old trap of representation: the goddess Reason was an actress from the Opera. It was still a spectacle, it was just another image, and these were even more cumbersome than the others since they claimed that they were replacing images by life. Therefore everything they showed was superfluous, *de trop*, everything was ridiculous or obscene: the artificial stage-properties, introduced into such a ceremony, were an exact measure of the degree of spontaneity lacking.

Robespierre was doubtless being more faithful to the spirit of Rousseau when he instituted the feast of the Supreme Being. But these too were only plans: it was still a painter, David, who decided on the costumes and the movements of the crowd. His plan anticipated, *foresaw*, what the spontaneous decision of a joyous people ought to have been: "When they see the beneficent star which colors and enlivens nature, friends, brothers, wives and husbands, children, old men and mothers, all embrace one another and hurry to celebrate and adorn the feast of the Divinity... Meanwhile the cannon thunder: immediately the houses empty—to be guarded by the law and virtue of the republic. The people fill the streets and public squares, glowing with lively joy and fraternity. These diverse groups, decked out with spring flowers, are a living garden, with scents which dispose the souls of each to the touching scene... The drums roll; everything takes on a new form. The youths, armed with muskets, form square battalions around the colors of their respective platoons. The mothers leave their sons and husbands: they carry bouquets of roses; their daughters, who must never leave them except to go to the arms of their husband, accompany them carrying baskets filled with flowers. The fathers lead their sons, bearing swords, and both fathers and sons carry a branch of oak." Here again, the new cult *abolished images*, only to erect emblems of renewal. One of the contrivances of David was to set up for the ceremony an effigy of the old order: this was to be destroyed and succeeded by a second figure, epiphanic, creative, victorious. Robespierre, taking a lighted torch, would set fire to the statue of Atheism, which, as it disappeared, "would be replaced by the statue of Wisdom, revealed in all its splendor to the assembled people." The deceitful image burned away, and at that very moment a sovereign truth was revealed in all its glory. It was a magic operation, destroying evil through its effigy. "The monster has been totally destroyed,"

Robespierre proclaimed; "the monster that the genius of the kings had vomited out upon France. May all the crimes and misfortunes of the world die with it!" But iconoclasm, here, is accompanied by the appearance of a new visible form—a new idol. *An image dies; an image is born.* And the enemy of tyrants, himself obtruding in his ecstasy of virtue, seemed in his turn to be a tyrant. That day there was a murmuring of voices which prefigured the fall of Robespierre. "It was," says Aulard, "like an advance rehearsal for the scene of 9th Thermidor." The destruction of the spectacular emblems of the old order was itself a new spectacle, renewing the fascination (and the sorcery) of scenography.

Thus, while they wished to see the annihilation of all exterior forms, new forms arose. Rousseau had dreamed of a transparency of hearts, but even he, in defining his ideal, could not do without the images of Rome or Lacedaemon—except when it was the idyll that he used for his setting. The rhetoric of civic virtue evoked an ancient order, a distant horizon. Unable to put this transparency of hearts into *immediate* effect, they had to find it an appropriate setting, site it in an embellished past, and clothe it *in* that past. Claiming that it was achieving this ideal, the Revolution did not in fact manage to invent new forms. It drew on the repertoire of antiquity, on the images of the Greco-Roman universe towards which the intellectual opponents of the *ancien régime* had already turned nostalgically when they had realized that they could not introduce an original order. The comic aspect of certain revolutionary ceremonies arises from the fact that at the moment when it should have been possible to create afresh men limited themselves to an imitation of the past, reconstructed by the imagination. Instead of promoting an absolutely new reality they took as their model a theater of shadows. Thus, as it burst into the modern world, freedom immediately adjusted its appearance to accord with great legendary precedents.

In composing his plan for the feast of the Supreme Being, David probably had directly in mind the description of the Panathenaea, which were at that time an object of general admiration, from the then well-known book by the Abbé Barthélemy, *Le Voyage du jeune Anachisis en Grèce.* David's academic Neoclassical inspiration is recognizable. But the link between the Revolution and the Hellenic ideal was not accidental. Winckelmann, speaking of the Greeks, affirmed that there was a strong element of liberty in every manifestation of their art: "The people's way of thinking grew up through the idea of liberty, like a noble shoot stemming out from a vigorous plant."

However, Winckelmann's perspective was that of a historian, retracing the birth, apogee and decline of an admirable art. But could this ideal be lived again? Should such perfect canons of art be respected once again? Neoclassical taste, while it was fully aware of the extent of historical discontinuity, played with the idea of a Hellenic renaissance. Line engraving, statuary in the style of antiquity (Flaxman), the painting of Mengs, fascinated by the example of Raphael and Poussin: these were just so many attempts to break into the hypnotic realm of greatness. But in striving after grace and dignity *(Anmuth und Würde)* they most usually achieved nothing but insipid flatness. The architects (Adam, Soane, Nash), using simple geometric forms, were to be more fortunate with their "dreams in stone," creating anew but with their eyes fixed on the old.

There did, of course, remain a decorative style, merging with the *style Louis XVI*, and inspired from the motifs discovered at Herculaneum and Pompeii. Flaxman was to model most perfect, elegant figurines for the ceramics of Josiah Wedgwood.

There were some men, however, who thought that the imitation of antiquity proved nothing more than the impossibility of creating a true resemblance. They considered that it would perhaps be preferable to refrain from trying to recreate the living forms of Greek beauty, that by perceiving fully the distance that separated us from antiquity we could better recognize the irreducible difference that made us, not ancients, but moderns. Were we capable of renewing the spontaneity, the youthful immediacy, the carefree blossoming of Greek nature? Were we not destined to anxious reflection, to melancholy passions, to everything that precluded a calm acceptance of the present? Were we not obliged to turn away from this impersonal beauty, and search instead for subjective truth, seeking out the "characteristics" which distinguished the individual's uniqueness and desolation?

3

PUBLIC ENTERTAINMENTS

Rica, one of the Persians in Montesquieu's *Lettres Persanes*, was completely baffled by what he saw taking place in a French theater and naively confused public and performers. "Immediately after dinner everyone sets out in a group to act a kind of drama which I have heard described as a 'comedy.' The main action takes place on a platform which they call the 'stage.' On either side of this, in small recesses which they call 'boxes,' men and women act parts in dumb show: you sometimes see a young woman, afflicted with the pains of love, languishing helplessly, or another, more passionate, gazing hungrily at her lover who returns her gaze with equal ardor. The whole range of human passions is depicted in these faces and expressed all the more eloquently that no words are uttered."

An architect had to be a master of many arts, capable of building theaters and riding-schools, of planning and constructing opera sets and organizing public festivals. And he also needed to be something of a stage manager and producer, for the movements of the actors were largely determined by the scenery.

Francesco Galli Bibbiena (like his brother Ferdinando and, in the next generation, his sons and nephews) devoted his whole life to scenography. He also traveled widely in Europe and was commissioned to build several theaters: at Vienna, Nancy and Verona (for the Accademia dei Filharmonici)

Utilizing to the full the possibilities of perspective, Bibbiena created an imaginary space, a world of depth in which the imagination could freely create images of human destiny. These settings far surpassed the second-rate tragedies of the day, and could be better associated with the music of Handel, Rameau or Scarlatti. The opera, which was the subject of incessant controversy, was one of the great aesthetic ventures of the age; when we study eighteenth-century scenography we must never forget that its true function was to supply an appropriate visual setting for vocal music. We can, of course, enjoy the music of Mozart's masterpieces for its own sake, but this music is itself dramatic action, an auditory representation of changing events and emotions; in other words, even the musical language of the period was governed by its analogy with the theater.

Thus it is only to be expected that most of the leading minds of the eighteenth century were profoundly influenced by the theater. Whether they were actors or enthusiastic spectators, they found in the theater an essential revelation which made them aware of their own originality and creative potential. Like Wilhelm Meister (in other words like Goethe) they discovered in the stage play, in dramatic creativity, a token, at once real and symbolic, of the versatility and power of the human mind acting in absolute freedom.

Impromptu performances, however, were declining. With Goldoni the loosely organized *commedia dell'arte* began to be replaced by a *written* text leaving the actor little scope for improvisation—he now had to *learn* his part. Harlequin was being polished and refined into an acceptable lover and the gaiety of earlier times, trivial and crude but also entrancing, was tending to die out. With his *Teatro Fiabesco* Carlo Gozzi stands out as a nostalgic figure, but he failed to revive the dying genre. For some years more the buffoonery of Carnival time lingered on, together with the pranks of Punchinello on makeshift stages —Giandomenico Tiepolo's superb drawings of these scenes belong to the legend rather than to the reality of the genre. At the height of the Romantic period, Hoffmann recalled them and reminded his readers of the need for a lively liberating irony.

Throughout Europe kings regaled their subjects with festivals intended to work the people up into an ephemeral, illusory state of excitement on such occasions as royal weddings, births, coronations or victories. Voltaire, at Potsdam, was no less impressed by the local festivals than Parisians were with theirs. "It is virtually impossible to grasp the spectacle I have just been watching—a combination of the tournaments arranged by Louis XIV and a Chinese Feast of Lanterns. Forty-six thousand tiny glass lamps twinkled in the huge square, marking out the tracks very distinctly. Four troops of horsemen, or rather small armies of Romans, Carthaginians, Persians and Greeks, entered the lists and marched around to the sound of martial music; Princess Amelia was there, attended by the judges of the games, to give out the prizes, like Venus bestowing the apple..." In Paris there were fountains flowing wine, imitation triumphal arches, illuminations of the Seine, and magnificent displays of fireworks.

But the festivals that the people themselves provided for their rulers were far from reassuring. It seems likely that the Revolutionary mob felt itself involved in a large-scale theatrical performance and that the more ardent Revolutionaries saw themselves as actors playing heroic roles. Prieur's sketches depict lavish theatrical gestures which suggest a clamor of grandiloquent tirades. And when, at the ceremony held in 1792, commemorating the fall of the Bastille, a gigantic trophy of monarchical and feudal emblems was set ablaze, the flames of the bonfire were an allegorical representation, illustrating the great rhetoric of *signs* that had been the philosophers' dream.

PUBLIC ENTERTAINMENTS

1. Ferdinando Galli da Bibbiena (1657-1743): Interior of a Theater (wrongly supposed to be the Teatro Farnese, Parma).

2. Charles-Nicolas Cochin (1715-1790): Illumination of the Rue de la Ferronnerie, Paris, 1739. Print by J. De Seve.

3. Alessandro Galli da Bibbiena (1687-1769): Design for a Stage Set. Drawing.

4. Giandomenico Tiepolo (1727-1804): Punchinello at the Circus Swinging on a Rope. Drawing.

5. Claude Gillot (1673-1722): Scene from the Italian Comedy. Drawing.

6. Claude-Louis Châtelet (1753-1794): Illumination of the Belvedere at the Petit Trianon, Versailles.

7. Jacques-François Blondel (1705-1774): Decorations, Illuminations and Fireworks on the Seine, Paris, 1739, for the marriage of Louise Elizabeth de France and Philip, Infante of Spain.

8. Jean-Louis Prieur (1759-1795): The Burning of the Barrière de la Conférence, Paris, July 12, 1789.

9. Jean-Louis Prieur (1759-1795): Commemoration of the Fall of the Bastille at the Champ-de-Mars, Paris, July 14, 1792.

6

7

8

9

IV

THE IMITATION
OF NATURE

FAITHFUL IMITATION

Imitate nature: the precept is passed on from generation to generation. But what *is* imitation? And what *is* nature?

Nature: the word has a thousand facets, can be understood in countless different ways. In the eighteenth century the man who wished to prove that he was right would invoke nature; he brought nature in on his side...

Does this mean the material universe? The whole gamut of created things? The entire "system of objects contained within the bosom of the world" (Sulzer)? The century had a new awareness of nature. The physicists, geometricians and philosophers of the Baroque period had won their battle. The idea of an infinite universe had triumphed. Galileo's telescope had pushed back the limits of the universe. It was the end of the traditional image of a spherical universe, circumscribed, surrounded by the empyrean and the "motionless mover." Henceforth there was no spatial hierarchy: no "sublunary" lower world, no angelic heights. The high and the low had lost their analogical sense: nothing in the universe could symbolize the *direction* of salvation or damnation. All parts were equivalent. Other inhabited worlds and other intelligent beings could perhaps exist. The center of the universe could no longer be the earth, or Rome, or Jerusalem, or even the sun. Anyone, here or elsewhere, could rightly regard as central the point where he himself was, provided that he was willing to recognize instantly the *relative*, provisional character of his particular perspective. With Georges Poulet we must stress that the eighteenth century "remains a relativist century. Truth resides in a series of points of view, and the supreme point of view, the only one capable of embracing the whole cosmos, is the point of view of God. This does not prevent each single point of view from being true, or each isolated place and moment from being the center of a circle which envelops a small part of the whole

truth." Perhaps, in fact, the deity is present in every point of the universe, as the mystics had suggested in the famous definition according to which God is an infinite sphere whose center is everywhere and whose periphery is nowhere. Newton affirmed that "there is a Being incorporeal, living, intelligent, omnipresent, who in infinite Space, as it were in his Sensory, sees the things themselves intimately, and throughly perceives them, and comprehends them wholly by their immediate presence to himself." Whether God is distinct from space (as the Cartesians maintained), or whether space is a mode of the deity (as the Spinozists argued), space is nevertheless neutral, isotropic, homogeneous, no given point having priority over any other. Further, if there is no absolute center and no definitive periphery, each individual mind—as Georges Poulet has shown—may claim the right to organize the world according to his own activity, from his own point of view, justifying his own private interests, while acknowledging the interests of others. This attitude was to be of consequence, for homogeneous space lends itself to the measurement of speeds, masses, relationships: it therefore reveals laws of matter which can then be exploited. The calculations of mechanics were to allow man to increase and direct his forces. The "point of view" of the individual was not only the center for his abstract contemplation, but the support for his practical transforming activities.

The concept of neutral space therefore helped man to be successful in his material enterprises by the methodical application of reason. Man's "uneasiness" caused him to test his strength in many directions. In this way he entered a world which he tried to guide according to his own will, to construct according to his own values and interests; and in proportion to the growth of his knowledge he saw his powers increasing. Neutral space is technical space. This had been announced by the precursors (Bacon, Descartes), and this is what the eighteenth century was preparing to achieve. Industry and commerce established a systematic basis for the exploitation of nature. The profit anticipated would be obtained with even greater certainty if man dominated nature by wielding effectively the uniform laws governing natural phenomena. Even though man himself might be subjected to natural causality, the knowledge which experience gave him of causality would enable him to master it—to a certain extent only, of course, but sufficiently to enable him to show his power by increasing his visible wealth and well-being.

The domination of space was manifested in many ways; primarily in the most concrete way of all. Roads, in Europe and above all in France, were multiplied and made safer; intercourse developed between towns and the countryside. Men chanced their capital and won fortunes in trade with the Indies and in mining ventures. The more prudent hoped to gain wealth by improving methods of agriculture. Such enterprises serve to illustrate the utilitarian invasion of space by means of human labor. This general movement, prepared and developed by the Renaissance, but held back somewhat by the wars of the seventeenth century, now finally got into its stride, with an impetus that has been maintained into the mid-twentieth century. An economic and social force—industry and middle-class trading—already dating back for several centuries, at last found its true language, its most effective methods, its "mental equipment"—in a word, its *ideology*. Overthrowing the old feudal system of cadastral surveying, which still retained vestiges of a universe guided and ordained by religious and "supernatural" values, the successful middle classes tended to emphasize the value of land according to its yield, its cash return. The estimation of property values based solely on money therefore supplanted the cadastral valuation of properties which had been based on the "charismatic" function of overlords and priests. It was Tocqueville who observed that the eighteenth-century anticlericals were opposed less to religion than to the wealth of the Church; they begrudged the soil that the Church monopolized and its power as a political institution. "The French Revolution attacked religion... not because the priests claimed that they governed the things of the other world, but because they were proprietors, overlords and tithe owners in *this* world."

The expansion of knowledge became an act of *possession*. It had at first been hoped that the world would be illuminated in its entirety in the light of geometric thought. But the time came when it was evident that the physics of movement was not a universal principle of explanation. It could not explain life. However, the various thriving enterprises did not renounce their objectives; instead they changed their methods, assuming a descriptive or pragmatic positivism. They turned away from geometry to undertake the study of nature itself; giving up any hope of translating each and every phenomenon by a mathematical formula, they limited themselves to drawing up a highly detailed inventory of nature. The *Encyclopédie* is the principal witness to this effort. (We should also add the systematist, Linnaeus, the antisystematist, Buffon, and the *Universal History of Voyages*.) The knowledge accumulated by the Encyclopaedists constituted a record of man's resources: arts, techniques, objects. What did it matter if we had no knowledge of the laws which might or might not govern the interrelationship of objects. The objects themselves, defined clearly and in isolation, are just as useful to us. "Thus man will have established his proprietary right over objects. He marks them off clearly, divides them into groups, and fits them into a universal plan. In appropriating them for his own purposes he transforms them: he denatures them, so to speak. Possession of the object changes its nature. A tree that you possess is no longer a tree that you simply gaze at from a distance... It is this sense of possession which is the outstanding characteristic of the *Encyclopédie*, distinguishing it from the *orbis pictus* in which the Renaissance travelers used to note down the curiosities they had observed during their wanderings... The Encyclopaedists conduct man on a proprietary survey. See, this belongs to you. You never thought you were so rich. This is what the scholars have obtained for you. Now learn to enjoy it all" (Bernard Groethuysen).

Images were to play a very large part in this process of appropriation. Drawn, engraved, colored, the whole universe—as seen by the naturalist-proprietor—was enumerated in its species, in individual entities (for, says Buffon, imperceptible shades of similarity link the various species reciprocally). Zoological gardens and collections of curios multiplied throughout Europe. Plants themselves, not replicas of plants, were collected in the herbarium. Pictures in books were regarded as a makeshift. The "imitation of nature" entrusted to etchers and aquarellists, although it played an essential part in man's acquisition of knowledge about the realities of the earth, seemed to take place outside the range of aesthetic awareness. It was regarded as the work of the artisan, not of the artist—as mechanical work in which no intellectual effort need be added to manual skill. These imitations were offered for man's use, for his further knowledge. Was it possible to speak of *art* when considerations of utility were so predominant?

For the *artist* it was not enough to produce slavish imitations of nature: the object must also appeal to man's feelings, his sentiments. This constant aesthetic requirement of the eighteenth century regarded imitative genre painting, even that of Chardin, as a *low genre*. It was some time before Diderot discovered that Chardin's painting was executed in the painter's own words, not with colors, but with feelings. At first Diderot was enraptured only by the *magic of the colors* and the *extreme variety*. "It is nature itself: the objects come off the canvas, so lifelike that they deceive your eyes . . . To look at other men's pictures, I seem to need different eyes. To see Chardin's pictures I need only keep the eyes that nature has given me, and use them properly." Genre painting succeeded in creating a double of nature on the flat surface of the canvas. It was a mirror, astonishingly accurate, reproducing the most diverse natural objects faithfully, but directed towards "low, common, domestic things." The illusion of reality was so great that the critic immediately felt himself involved in the attitude of proprietor-*consumer*. There was no poetic reverie before these foodstuffs; instead, one worked up a positive appetite. "This porcelain vase is genuine porcelain; these olives are truly separated from your eye by the water they are swimming in; you can just take up these biscuits and eat them, cut this orange in half and squeeze it, pick up the glass of wine and drink it off, take the fruit and peel it, or the pie and slice it open." Faced with such perfect imitations, contemplation shies away; things do not count, at first sight, for the mystery of their presence, but for their functional value. Consequently Diderot, for whom poetry was essentially dramatic, not visual, expressed disappointment: "This 'genre' painting should be the painting of old people, or of those who are born old. It calls for nothing but patience and close study. It lacks all animation and shows little genius or poetry. There is a great deal of technique and truth—and nothing more."

There was at least a constant search for truth. This obstinately accurate painting stood in the same relation to poetic painting as philosophy stands to lyricism. It was painting by a philosopher, and *for* philosophers. And this was no small achievement. Diderot could not refrain from admiring a philosophy which accentuated unusual objects, unexpected details, seemingly irregular accidents. If one accepts that "nature produces nothing inappropriate," then nothing must be neglected; everything must be made visible by a power of observation that will grasp the living essence of objects, gestures, personal features.

Tradition had been resentful of the exact artist's meticulous attention to finical detail, to variations, to individual discrepancies. It had been maintained that such detail emphasized the obstructions to nature rather than nature's general intentions. "Nature," wrote Félibien, "is usually defective in individual objects, for during their formation certain accidents ordinarily deflect Nature from her true intention, which is always to produce a perfect work." The defect which the same author saw in "German taste" (probably thinking of Dürer) was that it accepted nature "as we usually see it, with its faults, and not as it could be in its purity." About a century after Félibien, Mengs voiced the same idealism with even greater precision: "The works of Nature are subject to many accidents; but the artist's eye acts freely because it is working on passive substances which offer no resistance."

According to this doctrine, Nature would be found by stripping away initially all particularizing detail, in order to perceive the general type towards which Nature tends—the true natural form which human whims and fashions, together with the inertia of materials, often contrive to thwart. This was the attitude of Reynolds in 1770. The artist, he says, "will leave the meaner artist servilely to suppose that those are the best pictures which are most likely to deceive the spectator. He will permit the lower painter, like the florist or collector of shells, to exhibit the minute discriminations, which distinguish one object of the same species from another; while he, like the philosopher, will consider Nature in the abstract, and represent in every one of his figures the character of its species." But supposing there were no "Nature in the abstract"? Supposing Nature were concrete and nothing more? Supposing Nature did not tend towards the simple, using simple means, but towards the complex, using complex means? This whole idealist philosophy, which justifies the removal of particular detail, would collapse. Reynolds had written: "Every species of the animal as well as the vegetable creation may be said to have a fixed or determinate form, towards which Nature is continually inclining, like various lines terminating in the centre; or it may be compared to pendulums vibrating in different directions over one central point: and as they all cross the centre, though only one passes through any other point, so it will be found that perfect beauty is oftener produced by Nature than deformity."

Mengs took up this notion of "central form," using it as one of the themes of his excessively purist idealism: "As perfection is purely ideal and not individual, Beauty is the visible, figured perfection of matter. The perfection of matter consists in its analogy with our ideas..." His intention is touching enough; in practice, the result is an elegant but insipid Raphaelism. This conception envisaged nature as a power which tended *imperfectly*, for each object and each species, towards a central type which art could conjecture *perfectly*. Diderot and Buffon, however, countered it with the diametrically opposed image of nature as a power of variation, of divergency, of individuation. Natural activities were no longer envisaged as a concentric force but as a "continual movement of flux," of varying expansions in which the energies of the original obscure fermentation of matter were developing. Consequently it was no longer an ideal *type* that would show the creative intention of nature; on the contrary, it was the *individual*, and even, paradoxically, the individual that we might consider as a "monster."

Nature was no longer conceived as a power directed towards stabilized "central forms." It was seen as a dynamic force, capable of effecting all possibilities, of creating every link in the great chain of being, throughout infinite time. In this conception, Nature aspires to create individual differences and gradations, not specific types; life is the manifestation of a power of differentiation, the continuously renewed resultant of divergent deterministic forces; and there is no Creator superior to the creative power of Nature.

4

FLEETING INSTANTS
OF TIME

"The painter," wrote Diderot, "has but one moment; he may no more record two different moments than two separate movements." The eighteenth-century painter accepted this condition willingly, for his aim was precisely to capture the fleeting moment, to make it perceptible to the senses. Brush and oils were too slow for this purpose: only pencil, gouache, chalk or water color, which must be applied rapidly and surely, were suitable for the representation of momentary, transient objects. Hence it is in the exquisite drawings of the period that we find the fullest expression of its particular insight and genius. The artist's keen perception, his lightness of touch and his constant enthusiasm indicate faithfully that his model is a loved object, caught and immobilized in a precious instant of time.

We must, however, be careful to remember that for the eighteenth-century connoisseur these drawings, which seem to us to be so accomplished and so *complete*, had the casual charm of the unfinished work. A drawing was always regarded simply as a sketch, as something preparatory to the finished work. The observer's pleasure lay in completing mentally, in a complicity of the imagination, the work that the artist had abandoned at a stage when the picture still appeared incomplete. The moment recorded in the sketch suggested some potential work still latent in the artist. And this practice of combining an immediate, lively representation of the object with the suggestion of a hypothetical masterpiece, temporarily postponed, eventually had such appeal that artists were often inclined to abandon their works deliberately before completion. Caylus explains the causes of this pleasure, but expresses disapproval of what he considers an extravagance: "It seems to me that, when a mere pencil line or brush stroke can be made to convey an emotion and make us feel how faithfully and forcefully the artist has reacted to the expression, the attentive observer with a lively imagination may draw pleasure and self-esteem from being able to complete mentally what has all too often been left unfinished. The difference, in my opinion, between a fine sketch and a fine picture is that in the latter the great painter shows the full measure of his powers and purpose, whereas in the former we ourselves complete what the artist simply suggests—and it is often all the more pleasurable and flattering for that very reason. The only disadvantage is the way in which a number of painters have let themselves be carried away by the pleasure of drawing. They have almost given up painting in order to concentrate entirely on drawing. They have succumbed to the temptation of dashing their ideas down on paper—and also to that of imitating nature slavishly in their landscapes and their representations of those other forms of beauty with which nature so cleverly delights the hearts of her admirers. Yet, no matter how dexterously these artists sketch, there is still no denying that they are indulging in an artistic licentiousness for which they must be censured." It is certainly true that Gabriel and Augustin de Saint-Aubin were almost exclusively draftsmen (and engravers); yet to their "licentiousness" we owe a delightful series of pictures, glimpses of daily life, in which, without detracting from their anecdotal truth, touches of free fancy enliven the figuration and lighten the picture as reality is metamorphosed into an imaginative representation. We have a foretaste here of those qualities in the drawings of Constantin Guys which fascinated Baudelaire: a celebration of the beauty of the transient object, the lyricism of the ephemeral.

These artists were trying to catch the very essence of femininity, not only the languorous grace of a nude body, but a woman's characteristic gestures, her movements and bearing, and the rippling folds of the voluminous garments then in vogue. With the witty suggestiveness of which he was a master,

Fragonard shows us a group of young seamstresses going to bed, and it might be a scene from some light comedy. Here, by posing them against the light, he is able to suggest their bodies beneath their nightgowns. Sometimes he depicts immobility, as in the sketch of a girl seen from behind, standing in a patch of tall grass. Her costume, her hair, the turn of her neck and head are sufficient to suggest an undercurrent of desire: the whole body of this sensitive girl clearly suggests a state of emotion or expectancy. In Gainsborough's picture, which also depicts a woman seen from behind, we touch the mystery of the woman's step, revealing the heel and ankle beneath her lifted skirt. It is the simplest of poses, in which we can sense that the woman is moving away from us; this unfailing intuition of the "general effect" is, as Reynolds once remarked, a special characteristic of Gainsborough's art: "...He had a habit of continually remarking to those who happened to be about him whatever peculiarity of countenance, whatever accidental combinations of figure, or happy effects of light and shadow occurred in prospects, in the sky, in walking the streets, or in company. If, in his walks, he found a character that he liked, and whose attendance was to be obtained, he ordered him to his house..." So it was, perhaps, with this chance passer-by.

The French philosopher Alain has stated succinctly that "this kind of drawing suggests the possibilities of movement latent in motionless forms, with a boldness that is almost impossible to define." This is precisely the impression imparted by many eighteenth-century sketches and wash drawings of reclining figures or intimate scenes: an impression not of rigid immobility but of suspended movement and of an activity none the less perceptible for being wholly internal, cerebral: the quiet breathing, the gaze concentrating on the book itself or upon the more distant horizon of the fictitious universe that the book has evoked. Of the woman in Fragonard's *Women Reading* who is listening thoughtfully, Claudel has written that "we can only see her blurred profile; her attention is fixed somewhere in the distance, on something behind the picture, as it were, belonging to the imaginary world of the book; she cannot decide whether to give in to her imagination or return to the world of reality, and she leans there on her elbow, as if against the balustrade of some enchanted lake... And the whole scene seems to be filled with the echoes of some unspoken phrase."

FLEETING INSTANTS OF TIME

1. Jean-Honoré Fragonard (1732-1806): Seamstresses Going to Bed. Sepia drawing.

2. Gabriel de Saint-Aubin (1724-1780): Artist and
His Model, 1776. Drawing.

3. Thomas Gainsborough (1727-1788): Woman
Seen from Behind. Drawing.

4. Jean-Baptiste Greuze (1725-1805): Madame
Greuze Lying on a Sofa. Drawing.

5. Jacques-André Portail (1695-1759): Woman
Reading. Drawing.

6. Jean-Honoré Fragonard (1732-1806): Women
Reading. Bistre wash.

7. Jean-Honoré Fragonard (1732-1806): Girl Seen
from Behind. Drawing.

THE PLEASURE OF THE EYE

*Although pictures by the Dutch and Flemish "little masters"
were sought after by most collectors,* genre *painting was regarded in
the eighteenth century as a minor exercise. Acclaim and admiration
were reserved for* history *painting, which "embraced at once all
forms of nature, all its effects, and all the emotions that man can
experience." Genre painters, on the other hand, were considered artists
of limited ability, artists who resorted to depicting "particular objects"
because they were incapable of "taking in the full compass of art"
(Watelet). Nothing dramatic was to be expected from them, no
eloquence of expression, no moving or astounding events. These painters,
who move us so deeply today, were thought to be incapable of expressing
emotion, to be mere artisans, imitators of a commonplace reality,
uninspired technicians.*

*But these were fortunate limitations, for they led the painter to
revel in the beauty of ordinary objects and bodies bathed in light.
These pictures which scarcely do more than suggest a possible anecdote are
rich in implication. The girl's letter is most certainly a love letter, but
the painter, in catching the girl's expression, has recorded an intimate
moment of real life. How profound, how memorable a silence in such
pictures, after the frenzied activity of battle scenes, festivities and
representations of mythological events! Even when its theme is the
wiles of a Venetian procuress, this painting of reality excludes the
slightest whisper and allows the observer to concentrate solely upon
the visible appearance of things.*

*It is in this world of silence that Chardin is at his best: the gaze
of the silent boy intent on his fragile castle of cards, the little girl's
sidelong glance at the mirror. But to emphasize sight and seeing Chardin
does not need to depict human beings. With him things are not only
seen, but see: they answer our own gaze. We need only think of all
those surfaces glowing with a variable light, bright or subdued: fruit,
fur, glasses, copper utensils. "This is a harmony which leaves nothing
to be desired. It winds through the composition imperceptibly, fully
present in every detail of the canvas. As theologians say of the spirit,
it can be felt in the whole yet remains hidden at every point" (Diderot).*

JEAN RAOUX (1677-1734). YOUNG WOMAN READING A LETTER. LOUVRE, PARIS.

JEAN-SIMÉON CHARDIN (1699-1779). THE CARD CASTLE, ABOUT 1741. OSKAR REINHART COLLECTION, WINTERTHUR.

PIETRO LONGHI (1702-1785). THE LETTER. THE METROPOLITAN MUSEUM OF ART, NEW YORK. HEWITT FUND, 1912.

JEAN-SIMÉON CHARDIN (1699-1779). THE MORNING TOILET, ABOUT 1740. NATIONALMUSEUM, STOCKHOLM.

JEAN-ÉTIENNE LIOTARD (1702-1789). PEARS, FIGS AND PLUMS, 1782. MUSÉE D'ART ET D'HISTOIRE, GENEVA.

THE SECRET OF THE HUMAN FACE

Since the constant tendency of nature is to create diversity, since its infinite power is shown in the infinite variety of its products, we may grasp its fullness in the multiplicity of the human face. There is an endless variety of faces, characters, similarities and dissimilarities. No leaf from a tree is absolutely identical with another leaf from the same tree, noted Leibnitz: no human face has exactly the same features as any other face. The eighteenth century is the great century of portrait painting because of its sense that nature has endless resources, never repeats, and is satisfied only when it has created differently; and, at the same time, because of the conviction that every known certainty proceeds from the effort of an outstanding, independent mind, originating in an individual act, in a living presence which possesses the privilege of organizing the world as if from a central point (with the proviso that it must grant reciprocally the same relative supremacy to every other mind). Countless faces, and also countless different states, a succession of dissimilar instants captured in each face. If our life is composed of sensations, of anxieties, of passions, of acts of will shifting and changing with the variations of the world, each individual is a crowd, a host of successive dissimilar beings. Looking at the portraits of La Tour we encounter expressive moments, creasing half-smiles, imminent bursts of repartee. On a prepared basis of the firm underlying bone structure, the pallid substance of the pastel, in spite of its dull false-light and its artificially made-up appearance, succeeds in producing the impact of a real presence: the transient being has been captured in the very act of changing. Eloquent faces, too eloquent, caught on the very point of speaking, just about to confess, or to flash out a quip: the witticism, already thought, scarcely withheld, illuminates the features and is voiced in silence. (On the other hand, attention has been drawn to the portraits painted by Perronneau, in which the characters, with placid, happy features, seem to be "listening to music.")

This variety of expressions in La Tour, as in all the portraitists, is perhaps not quite the variety of nature. It seems to be, if anything, a repertoire of social mimicry, a comedy in a hundred different acts, a masked parade in which the mask and the face are one. Do these flickering, changing features disclose the multiplicity of souls, or the exquisite flexibility of manners? Do these portraits not reveal in their detail the uniform empire of taste, of good breeding, of bantering wit? These characters all inhabit a similar world, a French-speaking world, delighting in conversation.

In dealing with men it is always necessary to bear in mind the ways in which they deflect truth: with stiffness and pomp, when they wish to assume an air of permanency; with grimaces, simpering, sulkiness, the whims of fashion, the false mobility which parodies spontaneous movement. The visible features—the features presented for imitation—are tainted with artifice. Copy them faithfully, and you fall into the trap of deceit. Should the portraitist not, in the very name of art, imitate something other than the momentary appearance of his model? Diderot thought so and he reproached La Tour on grounds similar to those which led him to criticize Chardin: "In the works of La Tour we have nature itself; we have the system of natural imperfections as we see them every day. This is not poetry, it is only painting... La Tour has never produced anything spirited. He has the gift of technique: mechanically he is excellent."

But it is surely strange that one of the most ardent supporters of the particular imitation of nature should have pouted before paintings which depicted "nature itself." Is it possible that too faithful a resemblance displeased him? That he thought the details superfluous? Could he, like so many of his contemporaries, have mistrusted "individual truths"? In the *Encyclopédie Méthodique*, the section headed *Vrai* (composed by Robin) may occasion some surprise: "Pigalle has been justly accused of copying slavishly the heavy swollen corpulence of Marshal de Saxe. Well-built proportions and vigorous, clear-cut forms would have painted for posterity both the soul of the warrior and the agile, robust physique with which history will endow him in its descriptions." He appeals for a pious falsification in the interests of a *moral* truth accidentally betrayed by the corpulence of the great soldier: so art should reinstate an original *essence* now deformed by age and inelegance; make Henri IV a few inches taller, give Voltaire back his youth. Under *Portrait*, in the same encyclopaedia, the author begins by recommending that one should retain the details which "characterize the individual difference" of a head, then goes on to say that one should keep to the "general effect," to the idea of a face: "In this way, everything is ideal, everything is magical in art. Art introduces falsehood even into the most precise expressions of truth; it fascinates the onlookers, and to offer them the representation of an object it makes even greater use of the prestige of exact imitation." In order to do better than La Tour, it would appear necessary to acquiesce in this idealizing deceit which effaces, or deliberately exaggerates, or passes from the over-meticulous "mold" to the expressive idea. What Diderot desired, and with him a whole section of the public, was not the disappearance of detail, but the immediate transference of the detailed face, understood as a "visible object," as an observable "thing," into a system of eloquent significations. Diderot considered that the moral sense of La Tour's paintings was weak or artificial. This is what prevented Diderot from praising Chardin and La Tour fully: despite his encyclopaedist's passion for material inventories, he needed to be able to perceive meaningful *discursive sense* beyond the actual material object; he could not be satisfied merely with mute physical presences, however fine. Chardin, who painted the mystery of presences, evoking simple presences with the substance and light of objects, could not project the *discursive meaning* capable of arousing intellectual emotion. (At this period, when great poetry was considered to depend solely upon the development of dramatic situations, Chardin was actually protecting the chances of another form of poetry which had not found its *literary* expression in the eighteenth century.) The convention was to muse on representations of characters and passions —and if possible, of great characters and great passions—and it went against the grain not to come across events, even in portraits. This taste undoubtedly derived, throughout the century, from the prevailing interest in the genre that was considered superior: the depiction of historical scenes. For it was history painting (scenes from mythology, or from ancient or modern history) that presented heroes engaged in great actions: it was in these faces, as in the faces of actors, that the eighteenth century sought the sublime imitation of the particular passions aroused by a given event. They saw in this supreme genre the synthesis of all the powers of painting: "The history painter embraces simultaneously all the forms of nature, all its effects, and all the mental states that man can experience." A large elaborate setting would send the thrill of poetic appreciation through the soul of the observer.

For Diderot who represents the sensibility of all his contemporaries, the subject painter "is purely and simply an imitator, reproducing a common nature"; the history painter, on the other hand, "is so to speak the creator of an ideal poetic nature." Historical paintings organized a vast spectacle, a superb pantomime: could they be called illusory, when they were capable of illustrating the truth of the great movements of the soul? This is why the author, in the *Encyclopédie Méthodique*, faithful to the precepts of Reynolds, suggested that portraitists should school themselves with historical subjects: "Even if portraits are themselves deceiving, they could never be better handled than by those artists who, by practising in the historical genre, have familiarized themselves with the great deceits of art."

History painting, like theatrical gesture or intonation, was dominated by a rhetoric of passion. If it was sometimes felt necessary to revise certain of its precepts, no one thought of questioning the necessity of the rhetoric itself. They argued about the best ways of expressing fury, pleasure, uneasiness, gratitude; but no one even thought of disputing the convention that a picture had no merit whatsoever unless it represented such emotions suitably and accurately. Artists were free to ignore the particular kinds of passion drawn by Le Brun, but they could not escape from the general obligation of giving visual form to a typology of the passions. Although Diderot willingly acknowledged the infinite variety of subtle distinctions which differentiate forms, beings, or states of mind, he remained committed (together with all his contemporaries) to a psychological system which had established a limited catalogue, *ne varietur*, of human passions and faculties, according to an accepted classification. Regarding the products of nature he was loath to draw up a typology of forms, while for human emotions he could never rid himself of the traditional typology of affective feelings.

Any features worthy of pictorial reproduction should in fact, according to Diderot, comprise simultaneously the maximum of individuality and the maximum of typological expressiveness: "An actor ignorant of the art of painting is a poor actor; a painter who is not a physiognomist is a poor painter. In every part of the world, each land; in every single land, each province; in every province, each town; in every town, each family; in every family, each individual; in every individual, each instant has its particular physiognomy, its expression." Could one wish for a better statement of the principle of individuation? But here Diderot introduces the idea that the sentiments expressed in the painting must be absolutely clear and unambiguous; he expects the painter to have an infallible insight into the variations of the human soul; the artist must only depict sentiments that are perfectly clear, immediately identifiable: "The man bursts out in anger, or he is attentive, he is curious, he loves, he hates, he despises, he disdains, he admires; and every movement of his soul is to be depicted on his face in *clear*, *evident* characters that we *cannot possibly misconstrue*... A painter's expressions are weak or false when they leave the observer uncertain about the sentiment expressed."

Diderot is here formulating a program for a study of the pathognomy of the passions and the physiognomy of character. The basic language of signs, mimes or gestures, anterior to spoken language, also has its vocabulary. Lavater and Gall, each guided by quite different principles, drew attention to the conformation of the skull, of the forehead, of the nose, of "straight, curly or fuzzy hair," and followed the dangerous course that leads man eventually, as Hegel puts it, to make a bone of the mind. Just as Mesmer invoked the planetary influx mentioned by Renaissance philosophers, so Lavater returned to the doctrine of "signatures." But without going this far, and without "passing judgment on those parts of our face which our habits cannot change," Lavater saw good grounds for seeking out the impressions made on the human face by more or less constant occupa-

tions, thoughts or passions. Assuming that the most powerful passions were the most "natural" we could list the various elements of a universal language, always primitive but permanently valid, in which the statics and dynamics of the body would always offer a trustworthy calculation of the affections of the soul. In 1721, Antoine Coypel's *Discours* formulated this idea in accordance with a very old tradition: "The painter, in depicting attitudes and gestures, should not only compensate for the absence of words, but should also try to imitate the force of words and express those sentiments and movements of the soul which rhetoric teaches are necessary if we wish to be heard by all the nations of the earth." This search for a descriptive equivalent of the soul tallies with one of the great ambitions of the age: the analytical mind wished to survey all problems anew, in the perspective of life as it was *before* the growth of human conventions. They tried to isolate a basic, original nature, to reconstruct a language transcending frontiers, a universal dumb-show—literally, an authentic *language of action*.

Consequently, even those who, in the name of natural diversity, condemned the idealizing rhetoric of *forms* retained paradoxically a rhetoric of the *sentiments* which tended to establish uniform intellectual or emotional types. Whence the singular art, represented principally in the paintings of Greuze, in which the theatrical pathos of history painting was retained integrally. This pathos was now to be inherent in a realistic universe which acknowledged all individual variations in form. While traditional history paintings had presented ideal passions in an ideal nature, these same passions could now be placed in "realistic" settings which no longer excluded on principle singular details, such as—and primarily—details of social condition. This was an impure, crossbred art. It refused to idealize forms and objects, the better to idealize sentiments molded on a traditional psychology. The son is *ungrateful*, the betrothed is *shy*, etc... Since this art wished to combine the real presence of objects with the eloquence of great passions, it was often weak in both respects. For the depiction of striking distinctions of detail demands silence, while the spectacular depiction of sentiments requires an *economy* of detail, and even a visual transparency. But in these paintings we have both grand gestures and a multiplicity of detail. The middle-class world was striving after a spectacular dramaturgy that it was never to attain.

PORTRAITS

The optimism of the Enlightenment gave each man, provided he made proper use of the faculties with which Nature had endowed him, the right to challenge errors, deceptions and prejudices even if they were sanctioned by a long tradition of authority and obedience. By taming lightning, Benjamin Franklin put an end to the superstitious, supernatural interpretation of storms. But the originators of this new-found freedom had not intended it to throw individuals into personal solitude; quite the reverse, they meant people to be able to meet and know one another as absolute equals, their equality based upon their common reason. In affirming his own freedom, the individual was not to isolate himself within his own idiosyncratic personality: he would only experience the fullness of his freedom through social communion. In the eighteenth century, this accounted for the superiority of such arts as letter writing, conversation or portrait painting—the arts in which the individual defines, explains and asserts himself through the expression of his equal and reciprocal relationship with other people.

For the portrait painter of the mid-eighteenth century, the personality of the sitter was inseparable from his social function. The public insisted on the insignia of rank and position, so they were rarely omitted. The pastel painters, particularly La Tour, indicated a social human context less by means of exterior attributes such as clothes or décor than by catching the momentary expression, the fleeting mood and latent wit of the sitter, which always suggest the presence of another person outside the canvas. Alain says that "the fragile surface of the pastel lends itself to the essence of the drawing"; as a result "the colors always become artificial, like make-up, and the expression, too, is always fleeting and artificial. This is why a smile painted in pastels has no real depth, no sincerity; instead it betrays a self-confidence, a brash conceit that amounts to effrontery. So pastel portraits are always alike, as invariable as the hypocrisy and deceits of society."

And yet what gravity and simplicity portraits may have in the hands of genius! Mozart, close to death, contemplates immortality. Goya, immured in his deafness, catches the essence of his own troubled image; the time is approaching when communication will be increasingly difficult and consciousness itself will be anguish.

MAURICE QUENTIN DE LA TOUR (1704-1788). PORTRAIT OF MANELLI, 1752-1753. MUSÉE LÉCUYER, SAINT-QUENTIN.

JEAN-BAPTISTE PERRONNEAU (1715-1783). PORTRAIT OF JEAN-BAPTISTE OUDRY, ABOUT 1753. LOUVRE, PARIS.

WILLIAM HOGARTH (1697-1764). PORTRAIT OF ARCHBISHOP HERRING, 1747.
COLLECTION OF EDWARD HOLLAND-MARTIN, ESQ., OVERBURY, WORCESTERSHIRE.

FRA GALGARIO (1655-1743). MARQUIS ROTA AND CAPTAIN BRINZAGO DA LODI, ABOUT 1702-1703.
COLLECTION OF SIGNORA BEBE RADICI PEDRONI, BERGAMO.

JOSEPH LANGE (1751-1831). PORTRAIT OF MOZART, 1782-1783. MOZART MUSEUM, SALZBURG.

FRANCISCO GOYA (1746-1828). SELF-PORTRAIT, 1783. MUSÉE MUNICIPAL, AGEN.

CHARLES WILLSON PEALE (1741-1827/1834?). BENJAMIN FRANKLIN, ABOUT 1787.
FROM THE COLLECTIONS OF THE HISTORICAL SOCIETY OF PENNSYLVANIA, PHILADELPHIA.

ENERGY AND GENIUS

But this poor compromise was not the last stage of eighteenth-century thinking on the imitation of nature. One of the great lessons of "classical" idealism was to be thought out afresh, modified, stripped of its intellectual acceptation and given a new direction.

Perfecting the particular forms offered by the objective world, seeking in a multiplicity of imperfect objects the signs of a disturbed natural harmony, idealistic imitation had aimed to depict an absent model (which Reynolds situated in this world, not in a hypothetical hereafter). This effort to achieve a synthesis, this art guided by thought, had wished to produce a visible image of an invisible perfection. The work of art was thus the privileged medium for giving *sensory* form to a reality otherwise hidden from our perceptions. It introduced into the world absolutely new objects, the otherwise intangible reflection of the universe of essences, a veiled glimpse of "nature in general." Artistic beauty was therefore neither the exact replica of the tangible, nor an arbitrary invention: original creation aspired towards participation in the eternity of absolute forms, in the unchanging intentions of a nature deformed only by "accidents." As Reynolds saw it, the inspired mind would strive to transcribe an abstract perfection in visible form, correcting nature *by* nature. Some artists, who believed that only the Ancients had ever perceived the ideal, had taken them as their intercessors, their mediators.

But the image of Nature was changing in the eighteenth century. It was no longer considered as the great store of ideal types, but as a material dynamism, a continuously evolving energy, a fountainhead of tireless production. No longer a power in subordination to divine providence, Nature was herself becoming the supreme will, the unsurpassable sovereign power. The idea comes from the Renaissance and stems from a whole tradition of Aristotelianism, Epicureanism and Stoicism.

It was quite possible to exploit, in a materialist sense, the images of constant natural growth and of creative activity that Shaftesbury or Leibnitz had suggested. "O mighty Genius!" Shaftesbury had cried, "sole animating and inspiring power!... Thy influence is universal: and in all things thou art inmost. The vital Principle is widely shar'd, and infinitely vary'd: dispersed throughout; nowhere extinct. All lives: and by succession still revives."

Leibnitz, for his part, had defined the aesthetic act as an obscure power of the will enabling the intellect to "produce something resembling the works of God, though in miniature." Human minds, particularly artist minds, are not only "living mirrors or images of the world of beings, but images of the Deity itself, of the very author of nature, capable of understanding the system of the universe and imitating parts of it in architectonic samples, each mind being a kind of deity in its own department." If we accept that the omnipotence of nature dispenses us from the necessary hypothesis of a creating God, the analogy affirmed by Leibnitz seems to hold good. Are we not ourselves included in nature; and is nature not at work in us? Imitation of nature will not be simply outside observation of natural products: it will be stimulation by nature, participation in its movement, prolongation and completion of nature, creation *in the image* of nature by means of an aptitude granted *by* nature. Just as the idealist theory had advocated, an imitation of nature *from within* was considered preferable to a servile copy of external appearances: the artist was to participate in the "mechanical" reproduction of nature. So genius was no longer defined as a "light of the mind" (Félibien) and as intellectual talent: it was the activity, in man, of an obscure power of nature, a creative power which enabled nature to pursue its ends through the mediation of the artist. Genius, said Kant, is "that innate disposition of the temperament through which nature imposes its law on art." Instead of being simply an aptitude to think and seek the ideal true, from which we are initially separated, the quality of genius is in the actual presence within the artist of the supreme power, which is energy. "Energy is the only life; it issues from the body; and Reason is the bound and outward circumference of Energy. Energy is eternal Delight." Blake attributed this idea to the devil; but we should remember the German notion that it is only a short step from the genius to the "demoniac." This animation brings all our faculties into play, not excluding reason, knowledge, taste and intellectual intuition. We are animated from within, but this interior necessity coincides with our spontaneity, our most autonomous impulses. The language of spiritualistic philosophy (which spoke of innate ideas, divine enthusiasm) could be taken over in its entirety, provided one substituted *forces* for ideas, and *Nature* for God. Enthusiasm was not simply the ecstatic vision of a world of pure forms: it was a more ardent, a more obscure intoxication.

Consequently the *nature of the painter* now counted infinitely more than the nature of the external object he had chosen to copy. The object produced by the artist was not simply the replica of the pre-existing reality, it was a supplementary reality, a new fragment of the *natura naturata*. Diderot said: "Illuminate your objects according to your own sun, which is not nature's sun; be the disciple of the rainbow, but do not be its slave." Even in portrait painting, which is the imitative form *par excellence*, the painter was expected to develop an original power which would transgress, involuntarily but inevitably, the rules of strict resemblance. In the enthusiasm of his creation, the *gifted man* evoked by Diderot "strives in vain to copy faithfully" the features of his model. His freedom and knowledge, comprising rules which he has now forgotten, rules which have become unconscious (which "direct his brush without his noticing it"), lead him to modify what he sees: "For he has his own way, his mannerism, his color, to which he returns unfailingly: he effects a living caricature, while the dauber effects a moribund caricature. The dauber may produce a good likeness, but the portrait dies with the model; the gifted man's portrait remains for ever..."

The artist is therefore the creator of a reality which may then lead its own autonomous existence. The genius communicates life to whatever he touches. The end of the century was to see a rebirth of the myth of Prometheus, with all its implications of heroic effort and revolt against the prerogatives of the deity. In the event, it was not through the story of the Titan but through the fable of the sculptor Pygmalion that the eighteenth century chose to express the vivifying power of genius. It was an amatory, "galant" fable which could be told or represented under the pretext of drawing an analogy between outbursts of creative enthusiasm and bursts of sensual desire; a fable in which love was the symbolic means of surmounting the duality of the representation and the original, of the imitator and the object imitated: the artist and the work were bound together, merged erotically in an ardent embrace. No sacrilegious challenge in this story: the gods themselves were acquiescent. It could nevertheless be turned into a materialist fable: matter may come to life through love, a stone may awaken and become warm flesh; was this not a way of saying that there is no absolutely inert matter, that even marble contains potential energy and sensibility? This is what Bourreau-Deslande, La Mettrie and Diderot liked to think. According to their image of nature, all beings tend towards a higher, fuller life: minerals vegetate, vegetables tend to become animate, the superior animals to become human. How can man transcend himself, except by vitalizing every object that he fashions? Art need simply have the power to instill the decisive impetus into the particles of matter which are aspiring obscurely towards internal order, movement and life: the excitement of creative genius, communicated to the work, becomes warmth and pulsation. Painters and sculptors would evoke (sometimes rather insipidly) the marvelous instant of the first live throbbing, the first exchanged glance, of requited love. In the opera this would be the pretext for a tender duet, in which the statue was from the very beginning an actress draped in a thin veil. This fable expressed the optimism of the Enlightenment: the artist not only completed his general design successfully, but, bewitched by the perfection he had himself created, he saw the finished work, itself bewitched, now approaching its creator. It was the double fable of creative aspiration and fulfilled desire. Goethe, although he was entranced by its theme, criticized Rousseau's *Pygmalion* severely. He maintained that it was not good for the artist to marry himself off with his works: art demanded a certain distance, detachment, separation, not this warm loving complicity. To love oneself in one's work and to expect to be loved *by* the work was surely nothing but a virtually unmodified form of the deadly passion of Narcissus.

However, Goethe did in fact continue to maintain that the artist was the agent through which nature sought to produce her masterpieces. In order to transcend and contemplate herself, nature endowed man with the sovereign powers of creation, thus enabling him to perpetuate a beauty which, without him, might have existed for only a brief instant of time. Art was the means through which this fleeting natural beauty attained durable form. Man's exact observation of the world, together with the stylistic transmutation then imposed on his vision, constituted an operation in which man and nature conjointly achieved their salvation.

The work of art established an order which transmuted the passing instant into a timeless *presence*, a presence including and reconciling both the future and the past. Powerfully, mysteriously, the form held down the transient reality which might well have escaped us. Form, so defined, was not simply the imitative replica of an external model. The represented object itself, its singularity and ideality, had been a central preoccupation for too long: it was now necessary to realize that in the last resort the object imitated counted less than the creative act, than the power to *constitute* beauty of form. True singularity resided in the artist's mind; and, supported by the energy granted by nature, the creative subjective consciousness was aware of its solidarity with an impersonal power. Both singular in itself, and linked with the wider universe, the conceiving consciousness was not, according to Goethe, to abandon its function of mirroring the concrete world. Through the artist's private personality there was a profound natural energy advancing to meet the beautiful visible surfaces of the natural universe. The liberty of the creator, and the absolute authority of his personal whim, could not but rejoice at the idea of coinciding with universal necessity. Art was the human extension of the fecundity of the cosmos.

5

OBSERVATION
AND KNOWLEDGE OF LIFE

While painting the portrait of one of Alexander the Great's concubines, Apelles fell passionately in love with his model. The king's regard for his favorite painter was so great that he graciously made Campaspe over to him. For the eighteenth-century artist the *historical* theme of Apelles and Campaspe was not simply an opportunity for conjuring up the traditional scene of "the artist's studio." The image of the artist and his model took on a symbolical meaning according to which the painter became the rightful possessor of a Beauty which had previously belonged solely to the king. In granting this favor, the temporal power was acknowledging the special privilege of Art.

But the legend of Campaspe, and still more the myth of Pygmalion, implied that life (or the illusion of life) and the physical living presence of the object (or its simulacrum) are even more desirable than the creation of an imaginary world, a world of art in which *forms* are of paramount importance. The aesthetic governing these works is less concerned with a transposition or a transmutation of physical reality than with an imitative realism which would have us believe in the actuality, the proximity, of the bodies, feelings and gestures represented. Only the inertia of the artist's medium prevents us from deriving the same pleasure from these figurations as from the "realities" they represent. "How is it possible to express the idea of the statue changing into the body of a living woman? Surely, by endowing the head with life and thought and the body with the qualities of living flesh. But a fine statue possesses all these qualities, despite the fact that it is made of marble; if Pygmalion's statue had not had the godlike qualities of life and thought, he would not have fallen passionately in love with it. Thus the miracle which plunged him into an ecstasy of joy consisted in the metamorphosis of the lovely muscles of stone into muscles of real flesh" (Diderot). So it would seem that the artist's ultimate aim was not the artefact, however perfect it might be; instead, he sought to create an impression of real life, a sense of living presence to be induced by deliberate illusionism. Whether this presence was the model herself (Campaspe) or the physical incarnation of a perfect statue (as with Pygmalion) the artist's genius found its reward and happiness not in the work itself but in a flesh and blood reality. Instead of sublimating life to a new height of perfection in art, the artist was using his genius as a means of gaining the privilege of being loved by an attractive young woman. This propensity towards a hedonistic realism and the absence of any desire to create a world of independent forms account for both the charm of so many eighteenth-century works and their lack of creative tension.

The public wanted representations to be elegant and lifelike, faithful to the object perceived. The "Salons" at the Louvre (the first was in 1699 but, in Paris as in London, they became regular events only in the mid-eighteenth century) provided opportunities for judging, comparing and discussing the achievements of living artists. Here we have the beginnings of art criticism: impartial appraisals by writers or enlightened connoisseurs. Hitherto the right to judge works of art and pass verdicts on them had been reserved to the "Academies" (in other words, to the professional artists). Now such men as La Font de Saint-Yenne, Baillet de Saint-Julien, Bachaumont and Raynal made names for themselves in this new genre of writing, and with Diderot it was to achieve the status of a new branch of literature.

Diderot's sense of the relationship between art and life was exceptionally far-reaching and led him a long way beyond the commonly accepted ideas of the period. Nevertheless his appraisals of works of art, like those of all his contemporaries, are based on criteria which might equally well have been applied to actors and plays. He criticizes facial expressions, mimicry, postures or details of background in terms of the verisimilitude of the scene represented. When he discusses Falconet's bas-relief his admiration for the artist does not prevent him from finding fault with the innocent modesty of Campaspe's features: she looks too much like a "well brought up little girl... Her face is quite out of character."

This desire for truly lifelike reproductions was, of course, far from new. From Leonardo to Le Brun, painters had sought to establish the main principles of a *physiognomy of the passions*: and these principles could also be applied outside the sphere of art, to the interpretation of human nature in general. Can such knowledge be described as a true science? During the age of Enlightenment many French thinkers doubted if it were possible to extend to human "character" (that is, to the permanent structure of the personality) a system of knowledge which was properly applicable only to the "passions" (that is, the transient phases of a personality).

When, towards the end of his life, F. X. Messerschmidt carved his curious *Charakterköpfe* his object was probably less to represent general human types than to practise a sort of magical exorcism directed against the mischief of obscure phantoms. His uneasy mind resorted to mimicry, carried to the point of caricature, as a means of controlling the private dream figures with which he was so obsessed. According to the Zurich clergyman Lavater, facial appearance was a sure guide to the secrets of the human heart: God had willed that a man's character should be written on his face in a host of features or visible signs which an experienced observer could decipher and interpret. The *Physiognomische Fragmente* (1775-1778) included valuable contributions by Goethe and the engraver Chodowiecki. Goethe in particular collaborated in the chapters dealing with animals, writing portions of the text and providing certain drawings. As J. Baltrusaitis points out, the study of facial appearance in animals "is based on the same methods and criteria as those used in analyzing human beings. For example man's image, superimposed on the faun, reveals its character. The lively drawings depicting the faces of twenty-five apes —which could well be illustrations for a fable— strike a profoundly human note, precisely because they recall equivalent representations of man himself, the 'lord of creation'." Just as the stars in the sky hymn the glory of God, so the outward features of animals hymn the glory and supremacy of man.

OBSERVATION AND KNOWLEDGE OF LIFE

1. Francesco Trevisani (1656-1746): Alexander the Great in the Studio of Apelles. Oil.

2. Etienne-Maurice Falconet (1716-1791): Alexander and Campaspe. Bas-relief.

3. Etienne-Maurice Falconet (1716-1791): Pygmalion at the Feet of his Statue as it Comes to Life, 1761.

4. François Lemoine (1688-1737): Pygmalion Sees his Statue Come to Life. Oil.

5. Jean-Baptiste Pigalle (1714-1785): Bronze Bust of Denis Diderot.

6. Gabriel de Saint-Aubin (1724-1780): The "Salon" of the Louvre in 1753. Etching.

7. Henry Fuseli (1741-1825): Woman Looking at the Laocoön, about 1795. Pen and pencil.

8. Johann Rudolf Schellenberg (1740-1806): Apes, etc., engraving for Johann Kaspar Lavater's *Physiognomische Fragmente*, 1775-1778.

9. Johann Rudolf Schellenberg (1740-1806): A Device for Making Silhouettes, engraving for Johann Kaspar Lavater's *Physiognomische Fragmente*, 1775-1778.

10. Franz Xaver Messerschmidt (1736-1783): A Voluptuary. Marble.

11. Silhouettes of Goethe and the Young Von Stein, engraving for Johann Kaspar Lavater's *Physiognomische Fragmente*, 1775-1778.

6

7

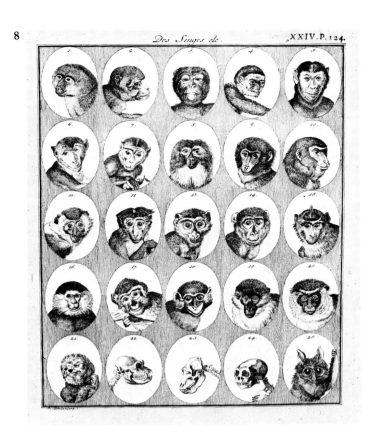

8

10

9

11

V

NOSTALGIA
AND UTOPIANISM

THE IMPOSSIBLE IDYLL

Festivals of joy proclaimed the union of hearts. Profound inspiration attested to the unity of genius and nature. Was it not therefore possible to imagine a higher synthesis, combining festivals and genius, social identity and the immediate presence of nature? This desire for a supreme unity obsessed certain great literary works—those of Rousseau and Hölderlin—but merely led to the judgment that this unity was unattainable. The more inspiring the desired image of unity, the more tragic and crippling was the destiny of those who had conceived it. For anyone dissatisfied with sham half-measures, the age was a call to arms.

In point of fact, as Schiller saw, the idyll offered a traditional *form* in which the dream of the great synthesis could first attempt to become reality. In the midst of a radiant or a lofty countryside, enveloped by the "maternal" solicitude of nature, men celebrated their alliance with the earth, sometimes by work resembling light-hearted play, sometimes by games in which poetry and music were shared by all and sundry. The song which then burst forth was the hymn of man and the hymn of the world, singing the harmony of man and the world. The eighteenth century had forgotten neither the Flemish *kermis* nor the heroic landscapes of Poussin: painters occasionally wished to reconcile the *extra-temporal* calm of the heroic countryside and the *actual* exuberance of rustic *bambocciate*. They sought the nice centerpoint at which the pastoral would receive the sharp tone of reality while retaining its limpid sky. They strove after an image of the universe in which all things would be governed by a fundamental confidence. We should remember that in literature the greatest reputations of the century were those of James Thomson and Solomon Gessner, poets of the simple life, of the seasons and their light. Men turned towards the countryside in order to contemplate it as they saw it, to live there in simplicity and good-will, supported by the powerful inspiration of nature. And they very often tried to abandon themselves to an illusion of rebirth: they wanted to return, if not to the legendary golden age and Arcadia, at least to a form of truth associated with basic elemental work, rugged confrontations, wholesome sober living. Perhaps this was even the way to regenerate society as a whole. It was, in any case, salvation for one's soul, by an escape from the corruption of the large towns and by setting up, beyond the shameful influence and scandals of the rich and the powerful, a small society governed by virtue, mutual understanding and justice. (Thus, in Rousseau's *Nouvelle Héloïse*, the *belles âmes* make the domain of Clarens a patriarchal state, subsisting by its own resources and governed by its own laws.)

However, in the event, this idyllic plenitude could only be achieved at the price of withdrawal, by turning one's back on the towns and their inhabitants. Theocritus himself, who invented the literary genre of the idyll, was a town-dweller anxious to escape from the corruption of the towns: to recapture a lost happiness he assumed a mask of bucolic naïveté. But could one now savor this simplicity again without perceiving an after-taste of pretense? It was only with an effort of the imagination that man could convince himself, in his secluded grove of trees, that the world was beginning anew and that virtue was triumphant. An attentive mind would quickly renounce the soothing pastoral flutes. He would realize that he was a runaway, that his acceptance of nature was merely the idealized expression of his rejection of men, and that he was playing all the various parts of the idyll by himself. Meanwhile vice was no less rampant in the town gutters... And in fact, an eighteenth-century art form, contrary to the idyll, was facing up to this vice, attacking it by exaggeration. While the pastoral denied the existence of corruption by creating an enchanted world, satire and caricature, for their part, were carrying out a work of negation by *overloading* the filth of reality. This was the antithetical complement of the idyll. The most striking example is the *Beggars' Opera*, which Gay composed on the suggestion of Pope, himself a writer of pastorals. This was a spicy parody of the pastoral, set in

Newgate prison, with brigands for heroes and prostitutes for heroines. The illusions of the pastoral inevitably brought forth an anti-pastoral, a " Don Quixote " of the idyll, designed to show the true sentiments of humanity, as opposed to bucolic idealizations. It was a concrete denunciation of the fanciful harmony in which privileged souls were seeking a complacent, illusory refuge. It denounced as unreal, as null and void, the particular image of happiness in which some men were tempted to believe.

In any case, the countryside itself, for those that had eyes to see, repudiated brutally any Virgilian dream that might be imposed on it. The realities of eighteenth-century country life would provide an inexhaustible inventory of misery, too painful not to contrast with even the most charming scenery. One need only consider the country folk of Giambattista Tiepolo, or, when they are not idealized, the country bumpkins of Greuze or Fragonard: the condition of the peasantry will not bear idyllic treatment. The countryside itself rejected such treatment wherever enclosures had been set up by proprietors who cared only for their yield and nothing for the meager resources of the poor. If "picturesqueness" was desired, it had now to be sought beyond these overcultivated fields, and beyond the regions where industries were being established. For man's successful industry, his iron and his machines, were eating away the natural countryside, disfiguring it. The traditional site of the idyll, no longer a theater of harmony, was becoming a theater of conflict. Another form of nature had to be sought out, intact, wild, remote, where men were scarcely to be seen. It was necessary to abandon social ideals, to become a traveler, an exile, contemplating the world in isolation. Though they did not turn away from the present, those who sought the secrets of nature were to turn away from mankind, for men were unfaithful to the old alliance, unsuited to the fair distribution of the gifts of the earth.

It is commonly asserted that in the mid-eighteenth century mountains ceased to appear "horrible." But it should be noted that the attraction of high mountainous scenery was originally justified as an attraction of the horrible. Previously, precipices had been hideous and largely uninteresting. Now, they were still hideous, but they attracted uneasy souls aspiring after the aesthetic emotion of terror. In addition,

it is quite probable that "picturesque" paintings in the style of Salvator Rosa played an important part in this revelation of mountainous scenery. The eye had been informed by paintings.

This shuddering before danger and eternal perspectives is perhaps not really different from enthusiasm. Are we not before the apotheosis of the sublime which, according to Addison and Burke, always contains an element of disproportion, the threat of impending destruction. Look! cries Shaftsbury in a text published in 1709, "with what trembling steps poor mankind tread the narrow brink of the deep precipices, from whence with giddy horror they look down, mistrusting even the ground which bears them, whilst they hear the hollow sound of torrents underneath, and see the ruin of the impending rock, with falling trees which hang with their roots upwards and seem to draw more ruin after them. Here thoughtless men, seized with the newness of such objects, become thoughtful, and willingly contemplate the incessant changes of this earth's surface. They see, as in one instant, the revolutions of past ages, the fleeting forms of things, and the decay even of this our globe, whose youth and first formation they consider, whilst the apparent spoil and irreparable breaches of the wasted mountain show them the world itself only as a noble ruin, and make them think of its approaching period."

This is a melancholy enthusiasm, teaching man his ephemerality, showing him that he is condemned to pass, as generations have passed before him, and that true wisdom resides in consenting to the alternances and vicissitudes that comprise the life of the universe as a whole. A man must give way to others, so that in their turn they may witness the sublime scene. What he meets on the summits is the dangerous face of that Nature from which genius draws its power. Nature unites him ecstatically with the idea of ruin and the passive cycle of the transmutations of matter. His delight is an acquiescence in death, an exaltation anticipating the arduous night in which he is soon to be immerged. And yet he might well have experienced the same shudder, with Young, by raising his eyes to the starry vault above a graveyard, or by contemplating ocean storms. The tempests of Magnasco, as later those of Vernet, speak of a nature which does not acquiesce in the tranquillity of the idyll. Here, the artist is no doubt rising to a kind of troubled sovereignty; he seeks our admiration by dealing with the hurricane as an equal; through the rapturous emotion of the color or the brushwork, he seems to aspire towards identification with the subject, to want to become a good conductor for the anger of lightning. The artist adopted the attitudes of the prophet or the damned, to bring us into the presence of the mortal fury that had fascinated him. The tempest in the epilogue of *Paul et Virginie* put an end to the last idyll of the century. Even if this cruel, savage, untamed nature were seen in a less fearful light, it would still exclude us, less by its violence and bitterness, than by our relative "denaturation," by the comparative weakness of our own passions. To some minds, poetic inspiration took its origin in the nostalgic sense of a broken contact, of a loss of vital strength. (Thus Faust at the beginning of his adventure.) The idea of decadence—which was to obsess so many minds in the nineteenth century—was appearing already. To the fearful sense of sublime disproportion, this added the awareness of a possible *fault*, connected with excess of knowledge, which could cut man off from his vital sources.

Thus, between the familiar world in which nature was damaged by man's industry, and the superhuman world in which a sublime nature revealed an eternity of overwhelming terror, there was no longer room for the bucolic myth of the union of hearts. And yet men were still attracted by the image of the pastoral world and by the taste for unity. So these ideals were so to speak reorientated towards a more distant, imaginary universe: the universe of death itself. A large number of eighteenth-century works are in fact pastoral dirges. Goldsmith's *Deserted Village*, Gray's *Elegy written in a Country Churchyard*, Gessner's *Der Tod Abels* and, to a certain extent, Goethe's *Werther*, are works in which the idyllic spirit is manifested for a short time only to reach the limit at which the internal requirements of truth and fatality demand the death of the idyll (if necessary through the deaths of the idyllic characters). Forced back into the universe of death and of past time, the idyll becomes the elegy, the "sentimental" poem of lament and nostalgia. Projected towards future time, the idyll widens and becomes Utopian, the imaginary elaboration of universal reconciliation. In both instances the spirit is dedicated to the contemplation of something lost in the past or in the future—something longed for, and unattainable. In meditating upon a desire which the actual world can no longer fulfill, the spirit aspires towards an absent ideal.

SIR JOSHUA REYNOLDS (1723-1792). ELIZABETH DUCHESS OF BUCCLEUCH WITH HER DAUGHTER, LADY MARY SCOTT.
THE DUKE OF BUCCLEUCH AND QUEENSBURY, K.T., BOWHILL, SELKIRK, SCOTLAND.

THE ENGLISH IDEAL

Reynolds, in his Third Discourse, *quotes approvingly from the Neoplatonist philosopher Proclus: "He who takes for his models such forms as Nature produces, and confines himself to an exact imitation of them, will never attain to what is perfectly beautiful; for the works of Nature are full of disproportion, and fall very short of a true standard of beauty." This precept held good not only for large compositions but also for landscape and portraiture, which were favorite subjects in eighteenth-century English painting.*

The English school offered the aristocracy a flattering portrait with all its imperfections quietly omitted. In contrast to the affectation of Nattier, luxury does not reside essentially in ornament, dress, or the décor of a salon; it belongs to a special beautifying light which covers everything it touches with the smooth skin of the ideal. Instead of being depicted in sumptuous salons, the models are placed in the open air, against the background of a flawless nature, a spotless creation. Every detail is transmuted and ennobled. The universe seems to contain nothing but delicate, composed, noble beings, surrounded by their faithful animals. In this rediscovered golden age, the comfort and ease of civilized life were to be experienced in the woods and meadows. Human happiness lay in taking full advantage of the family estates, with their deep groves and forests, with mysterious shady avenues along which the gentry could gallop in the morning mists.

Though he was a master in the art of rendering the natural scene faithfully, Gainsborough attributed an air of poetic happiness even to the children of beggars, as if the ideal universe must necessarily include the serene archetype of the beggar. Historians affirm that the enclosures, which facilitated the systematic cultivation of large estates, reduced small farmers to abject poverty. This human misery constituted precisely that "imperfect nature" which painters were urged to ignore or transcend. Therefore, although they were searching sincerely for a purified ideal of beauty, these artists created the stock image of a restful garden in which there was nothing to offend the eye. (The delusion inherent in this ideal image is revealed fully if one merely glances through the sketches of the caricaturists.)

THOMAS GAINSBOROUGH (1727-1788). ROBERT ANDREWS AND HIS WIFE, ABOUT 1748-1750.
REPRODUCED BY COURTESY OF THE TRUSTEES, THE NATIONAL GALLERY, LONDON.

GEORGE STUBBS (1724-1806). THE MELBOURNE AND MILBANKE FAMILIES, 1770.
COLLECTION OF J. J. W. SALMOND, ESQ., SALISBURY, WILTSHIRE.

Addison's comments in his essays "On the Pleasures of the Imagination" are fundamental to an understanding of the eighteenth-century sensibility. "By greatness, I do not only mean the bulk of any single object, but the largeness of a whole view, considered as one entire piece. Such are the prospects of an open champaigne country, a vast uncultivated desert, of huge heaps of mountains, high rocks and precipices, or a wide expanse of waters, where we are not struck with the novelty or beauty of the sight, but with that rude kind of magnificence which appears in many of these stupendous works of nature. Our imagination loves to be filled with an object, or to grasp at anything that is too big for its capacity. We are flung into a pleasing astonishment at such unbounded views, and feel a delightful stillness and amazement in the soul at the apprehension of them... But if there be beauty or uncommonness joined with this grandeur, as in a troubled ocean, a heaven adorned with stars and meteors, or a spacious landscape cut out into rivers, woods, rocks and meadows, the pleasure still grows upon us, as it rises from more than a single principle."

Pleasure in grandeur, mingled with a kind of "thrill of horror" or "terrible joy"—this is the reaction to nature which gave rise to what Marjorie Nicolson has aptly called "the aesthetics of the infinite." Through the infinity of the world around us we are made aware of the infinity of God. In turning to the sublime spectacles afforded by nature, the philosopher believed himself to be turning away from art and its all too human rhetoric. But a new generation of artists was intent on breaking away from hackneyed formulas and introducing hitherto unknown emotions; they sought to capture the wild sublimity and grandeur of untamed nature through representations of its tremendous majesty. A new aesthetic medium, a new current of taste, were thus created: and they gave expression to emotions which appeared to transcend human speech and defy the limitations of form.

FRANCIS TOWNE (1740-1816). THE SOURCE OF THE ARVEIRON, 1781. COURTESY VICTORIA AND ALBERT MUSEUM, LONDON.

JOSEPH WRIGHT, CALLED WRIGHT OF DERBY (1734-1797). MOONLIGHT LANDSCAPE, 1780-1789?
PALMER-MOREWOOD TRUST, ART GALLERY AND MUSEUM, BRIGHTON.

WILLIAM HODGES (1744-1797). TAHITI REVISITED, 1775. NATIONAL MARITIME MUSEUM, GREENWICH.

JOSEPH VERNET (1714-1789). THE STORM, 1777. MUSÉE CALVET, AVIGNON.

6

VIEWS

"The term 'view' is applied to the 'portrait' of a site, copied directly from nature. This genre covers a great variety of subjects: seascapes, cliffs, rocks, cottages, unusual stretches of country. Such studies, provided they are copied from nature, are called views. For great artists this is a relaxation, for they can depict such views with delightful ease. It is also a source of pleasure to those who watch them work so skillfully. Equally, this kind of exercise draws their attention to a wide range of objects, details and facts which never fail to catch the imagination and arouse their interest" (Watelet).

Views are therefore an exercise for the painter when he travels—unless of course they are drawn or painted by local artists for travelers who wish to have souvenirs of the unusual sights that have caught their eye. This genre of art is therefore bound up with traveling, discoveries, encounters with the unfamiliar, all the sensations of wonder and delight which we experience when we suddenly come across one of those caprices or oddities of nature which seem to anticipate the perfection of finished works of art. A scene which catches our attention in this way is commonly called "picturesque," meaning that it has a special charm simply "asking" to be converted into a picture. Thus Nicolas Cochin advises the painter "to note down in particular, when he travels, those species of picturesque trees that are rare in his own country. The French painter, for example, will observe pines and cypresses, trees seldom found in France. He will note how they seem to change color at various distances. He must take notes and make sketches of all these things so that he may remember them accurately; he must never trust his unaided memory, since impressions and ideas of this sort are very easily forgotten if he does not record them in some way." This was the practice of Fragonard, Hubert Robert and many others during their journeys in Italy. They were not interested exclusively in trees, rocks, lakes, rivers and "poetic" gardens; following the taste of their contemporaries they emphasized equally the work of human hands, "the superadded buildings which adorn the landscape." But to be "picturesque" these buildings had to be either "noble" (i.e. in ruins) or rustic (i.e. thatched cottages). "Ruined or Gothic buildings," wrote Levesque, "impart a sense of decrepitude which appeals to persons with a nostalgic turn of mind. Such people are fond of comparing nature, with its eternal youth and fertility, with the buildings erected by man, buildings which, however stoutly built, grow old and fall into decay. Noble edifices add majesty to a landscape, while rustic dwellings suggest the purity and tranquillity of their inhabitants, their ideal country life. Pictures of rustic cottages can be tastefully enhanced by including a few of the implements that country folk usually leave outside their homes: ladders, buckets, tubs, old casks, troughs, carts or ploughs. Cottages are all the more picturesque for being old and full of *character*."

Through constant practice in copying the picturesque (later described as "romantic") aspects of nature, artists began to make a habit of painting picturesque scenes. Whereas art had originally introduced the notion of picturesqueness in nature, artists now began to invent new modes of the picturesque, based not upon the natural scene but upon their own imagination. The painter considered that he had the right to create imaginary landscapes, since Nature herself was only beautiful when she imitated the "effects" of painting. With Guardi and Canaletto it is not always easy to distinguish between views, capriccios and purely imaginary landscapes. The patrons for whom they worked sometimes asked for exact imitations, and sometimes for hallucinating scenes of natural beauty, whether or not this meant departing from the truth. And one of Juvarra's sketches for a stage set shows that the imaginary landscape had much in common with scenic backgrounds. "Picturesque" landscape scenes are in fact simply theatrical versions of the landscape painter's "caprices."

Old cottages were considered picturesque because they gave form to a yearning for the frugal homeliness of peasant life, whereas caprices in the Venetian manner were picturesque in that they lent a discreet animation to districts of the city where life followed a regular, gentle rhythm. But towards the close of the century the picturesque came to be associated with the wildness of nature, with raging tempests and with the huge petrified movement of mountains.

In its turn, the picturesqueness of the fury of nature made painters wish to surpass nature: after imitating faithfully they took to inventing imaginary scenes. Thus Alexander Cozens excelled nature by creating fantastic landscapes, conjured up by his own imagination and unrelated to any existing landscapes. Technically, he resorted to a system of fortuitous "blot drawing" in which he used haphazard blobs of ink or color as guides or starting points for compositions which he then worked out in detail. This method was based on a type of "automatism" which gave visual form to the obscure movements of the imagination: it could be described as an *interpreted tachism* which, as early as the eighteenth century, had the value of the "projective test" which we now apply in interpreting modulated patches in certain modern paintings. Cozens expounded the system in his *New Method of Assisting the Invention in Drawing Original Compositions of Landscape*. He agreed that landscape painting should not be an imitation of nature. It was instead a means of giving representative form, through the imagination, to the general principles of nature. A simple "blot" on a sheet of paper would produce accidental shapes, masses unrelated by any line, but suggesting certain ideas. This, according to Cozens, was similar to the processes of nature, for in nature forms are defined not by lines but by the accidental play of light and shade. Since the same "blot" may suggest different ideas to different people, it follows, says Cozens, that this procedure stimulates the artist's inventive powers, and therefore gives better results than a mere study of nature. In Cozens' own painting the application of this theory had remarkable results, including a rediscovery of the secrets of Oriental landscape painting, with which he was familiar. In particular his monochrome water colors show nature in an original, hallucinating reinterpretation.

VIEWS

1. Antonio Canaletto (1697-1768): Imaginary View of Padua. Drawing.

2. Francesco Guardi (1712-1793): Playing at Dice on a Piazza in Venice. Pencil, wash and crayon.

3. Hubert Robert (1733-1808): Courtyard behind the Roman Theater at Orange, about 1783. Drawing.

4. Antonio Canaletto (1697-1768): Country House near a Town with Bell-Towers in the Distance. Drawing.

5. Francesco Guardi (1712-1793): The Bridge of Sighs and the Ponte della Paglia, Venice. Drawing.

6. Filippo Juvarra (1676-1736): Stage Scenery for *Cyrus* (1712) at the Teatro Ottoboni, Rome. Drawing.

7. Jean-Honoré Fragonard (1732-1806): Neptune's Grotto at Tivoli, about 1760. Red chalk.

8. Jean-Honoré Fragonard (1732-1806): View of the Italian Coast near Genoa. Drawing.

9. Alexander Cozens (1716-1786): Mountain Landscape. Drawing.

10. Alexander Cozens (1716-1786): The Cloud. Drawing.

4.

5

6

7

8

9

10

MELANCHOLY AMONG THE RUINS

Poetry may give expression to *absence*, but is this possible for the visual arts, which are arts of presence? Is it possible for painting to be elegiac? Can it give the pastoral, not the eternal light of classical beauty, but the heart-rending quality of loss? In painting it is hazardous to try to evoke a sense of *completed time*. There is, however, one constant resource, which is to rely on objects whose very presence suggests some forgotten age. This effect is inherent in ruins. Ruins were a favorite theme to eighteenth-century sensibilities, but, like many intellectual fashions, it was simply a renewal. Petrarch, one of the first men to dream of a "renaissance," a rebirth, described his walks amongst the vestiges of the greatness of Rome. Very soon, as Waetzoldt points out, painters had recourse to ruins as an intermediary setting between man-made structures and the natural world, between the palace and the rock. The *Hypnerotomachia Polyphili* is an amorous quest among the ruins, as was, later, Jensen's *Gradiva*, which has been analyzed by Freud. It is widely known that for the painters of the Quattrocento the martyrdom of St Sebastian had almost necessarily to be situated against a background of ruins. Ruins were to figure constantly in the Orient background to nativity scenes, symbolizing at once the mystery of the country and the old alliance now surpassed by a new faith. Soon the famous ancient monuments (obelisks, the Colosseum, the Temple of the Sibyl at Tivoli) became figurative accessories which painters distributed as they thought fit. Claude Lorrain did not hesitate to erect the Arch of Constantine on the banks of a river. And even those who had never seen Rome borrowed the image of the ruined temple from collections of prints, to give *interest* to a scene. Vestiges of the past ennoble nature, make commonplace country scenes *heroic* or *idyllic*. And just as the memory of Salvator Rosa's precipices drew the "connoisseurs" to the Alps, so the memory of Claude's temples guided them towards the Campo Vaccino; when the young English aristocrats made their "grand tour," this was an obligatory visit. In flight from their island *spleen* they sought out this satisfying relapse into melancholy, but it was now transformed into a noble, disinterested melancholy, under the bright skies of Italy!

Painters and engravers were at work for these travelers. Otherwise what would have remained of the hours spent in contemplation of the famous places? On their return, the richer travelers hung their rooms with large painted *vedute* of the Forum or the Pantheon; the less wealthy made do with local prints. (This industry has now been replaced by the sale of postcards.) Pannini excelled in the genre. In his youth he had drawn architectural decorations; from there it was a simple matter to pass on to wider "perspectives" and *vedute*. Goethe looked on these as landscape-portraits (Porträtlandschaften) which could be varied according to three principal types: the panorama, the grand motif, and the close, intimate view. Pannini himself did not hesitate to group together on a single canvas a whole collection of interesting sights which were in reality far distant from one another. It was much like reuniting distant cousins for a family portrait. The lover of antiquity could then gaze on the condensed summary of all the vestiges of ancient Rome.

With the Venetian Giambattista Piranesi, the art of the *veduta* reached its greatest heights. Proud of his abilities as an architect, he was haunted by a somber dream whose heroes were creatures of stone. He had loved Rome passionately, and he reproduced it, transfigured, with the ghostly majesty of a power determined to resist decay. With his precise drawings and hallucinating artist's vision, he so handled lights and shades that he gave stone an expressivity that had scarcely existed before him. Goethe, with his predilection for the ideal of classical balance, openly confessed his uneasiness before the "richness of effects in this Rembrandt of the ancient ruins." To the fiery enthusiasm of Piranesi Goethe preferred the more restrained, more discreet work of Hermann van

Svanevelt. It is true that Piranesi, exaggerating the effect of certain perspectives, developed a disproportionate universe in which monuments, a symbol of destiny, infinitely surpassed the human form: beside the great shades haunting the ancient structures, purely human gestures fall away into insignificance. Goethe, who so ardently desired to emphasize the human, could not accept this solemn condemnation of the present by the past.

In fact, in its calmer form, and provided it does not go so far as the anxiety of a Piranesi, the aesthetics of the ruin can express a minor form of idyll: a new union of man and nature, through the intermediary of man's resignation to death. "The charm of the ruin," writes Georg Simmel, "resides in the fact that it presents a work of man while giving the impression of being a work of nature... The upward thrust, the erection of the building, was the result of the human will, while its present appearance results from the mechanical force of nature, whose power of decay draws things downwards. However, in so far as one can speak of ruins, and not just of piles of stones, nature does not allow the work to fall into the amorphous state of its raw material. A new form is created which, from the point of view of nature, is of the greatest significance and is perfectly comprehensible and differentiated. Nature has used man's work of art as the material for its own creation, just as art had previously taken nature as its raw material.

"Consequently, the ruin gives an impression of peace, because in it the opposition between these two cosmic powers acts as the soothing image of a purely natural reality. This explains why a ruin is easily assimilated into the surrounding countryside, why it lies there like a stone, or takes root like any tree, whereas a palace, or country house, or even a peasant's cottage, no matter how well they may be adapted to the character of the countryside, always suggest another order of reality and only later seem to fit in with the purely natural order." Thus, in this involuntary evolution, the original upward movement of art is harmonized with the natural forces of descent and inertia. A balance is achieved in which the opposing forces of nature and culture are reconciled as man moves on, when the traces of human effort are fading away and the natural wilderness is regaining its lost ground. The material forms which bear witness to the greatness of an age have not given way completely to ageless confusion. The traces of a

grand design survive; but the surest survival is that which the moss and the wild undergrowth betoken, a survival which obliterates all earlier human intentions, remains which represent oblivion. The poetry of ruins is always a reverie before the encroachment of oblivion. It has been pointed out that for a ruin to appear beautiful, the act of destruction must be remote enough for its precise circumstances to have been forgotten: it can then be imputed to an anonymous power, to a featureless transcendent force—History, Destiny. We do not muse calmly before recent ruins, which smell of bloodshed: we clear them away as quickly as possible and rebuild. We pour out our anger against an aggressor who can be named. The poetry of ruins is the poetry of what has partially survived destruction, though remaining lost in oblivion: no one must retain the image of the intact building. The ruin *par excellence* indicates an abandoned cult, a forsaken god. It expresses neglect, desertion. The ancient monument had originally been a memorial, a "monition," perpetuating a memory. But the initial memory has now been lost, to be replaced by a second significance, which resides in the disappearance of the memory that the constructor had claimed he was perpetuating in this stone. Its melancholy resides in the fact that it has become a monument of lost significance.

In the history of European sensibility the theme of the country churchyard was contemporary with the theme of the ruin. It indicates the same tendency towards ineffectual reminiscence, the same helpless effort of memory, scrutinizing oblivion without mastering it. These obscure destinies, now eternally effaced, symbolize a mystery inaccessible to the light of human consciousness.

But awareness of this oblivion implied awareness of the necessity of remembering. Musing over the slumbering stones, the ruins with their roaming goats, the imagination became more objective, the mind became questioning, the questions gave rise to a methodical inventory: the ruins were related to their spatial and temporal coordinates. It is well known that historians have found their vocations while contemplating ruins. Witness Gibbon: "It was at Rome on the 15th of October 1764 as I sat musing amidst the ruins of the Capitol, while the bare-footed friars were singing Vespers in the temple of Jupiter, that the idea of writing the decline and fall of the city first started in my mind." Before Gibbon, and after him, the "antiquarians," scholars and archaeologists of the eighteenth century questioned the old remains and tried to reconstruct a credible picture of the past. Even Piranesi's imaginative monuments were taken to be systematic accounts; works of the imagination began to appear scientific. When men reached the stage of deciphering the names of the forgotten gods, of unearthing ancient vases, it was the end of the ambiguous poetry of the ruins, for its cause, a sentimental ignorance, had been removed. Those who remained attached to their sentimental emotion considered that it was a sacrilege to *date* things which should impart a sense of the *immemorial*. In the eighteenth century emotional feeling for ruins had to compete against the awakening of modern historical thinking, which gradually depoetized the ruins as its investigations became more methodical. The work of Volney is a striking witness to this evolution. And, as one of Goethe's friends wrote, what is won for erudition is lost for the imagination: "Antiquity should appear to us only in the distance, separated from everything that is commonplace: it should appear purely as a bygone age... Only with the divine anarchy of Rome itself, and only with the heavenly isolation around the city, can there be place for the shades of the past; and a single one of these is worth more than the whole of the present generation." To enjoy the past poetically, the lover of antiquity liked to fancy that the present was nothing if not cankered.

ALESSANDRO MAGNASCO (1667-1749). SOLDIERS AND GIPSIES IN RUINS, 1710-1720. COUNT FAUSTO LECHI COLLECTION, BRESCIA.

THE CONTEMPLATION OF TIME

The painting of ruins constituted a well-defined genre between architectural painting and landscape. While Canaletto painted palaces and towns, Pannini and Hubert Robert turned to the poetic vestiges of the great buildings of ancient Rome. Hitherto—as we see from the canvas by Magnasco reproduced here—ruins had been included only for their scenic value; to the spatial depth of the picture they added a temporal dimension; the present moment was sustained by the rugged persistence, the continuity of the past. But now the ruins were brought into the foreground to become the main theme of the picture; they were depicted for their own sake, for that obstinate resistance to the ravages of time which made them almost like some heroic figure, advanced in years but strong-willed as ever.

In Pannini's work, however, the documentary aspect of the subject does predominate; his intention was simply to remind his contemporaries of the architectural achievements of an illustrious past. To gratify his patrons he often brought together on a single canvas widely scattered monuments, and the pictures resemble museum collections. But sometimes he allows his imagination free rein: strolling through the arches of a bygone age, his eighteenth-century figures seem to be moving in a dream. Diderot comments as follows:

"Great thoughts stir within me at the sight of ruins. Everything gradually crumbles and vanishes. Only the world remains. Only time endures. And how old the world is! I am walking between two eternities. Whichever way I turn my eyes, I see objects that have perished—and am reconciled to my own end. What is my own ephemeral existence in comparison with the age of this valley scooped out between the walls of crumbling rock, this quivering forest, or these trembling masses swaying above my head? The very marble of the tombs falls away into dust; and I do not want to die! . . . A torrent hurls nations in tangled disarray into the depths of a common abyss; while I, and I alone, have the presumption to halt on the brink and cleave the waters flowing by me!"

FRANCESCO GUARDI (1712-1793). CLASSICAL COMPOSITION: RUINS AND FIGURES. COURTESY VICTORIA AND ALBERT MUSEUM, LONDON.

GIOVANNI PAOLO PANNINI (1691/1692?-1765). RUINS. GALLERIA CORSINI, ROME.

GIOVANNI NICCOLO SERVANDONI (1695-1766). RUINS, 1731. ECOLE DES BEAUX-ARTS, PARIS.

HUBERT ROBERT (1733-1808). RUINS OF A ROMAN TEMPLE, 1780? MUSÉE CALVET, AVIGNON.

GOTHIC TALES

If, instead of being mitigated by a resurrection in nature or in learning, death remained irreducible, the presence of shadows amongst the ruins could be heavy with foreboding. Melancholy contemplation would develop into apprehension, into dread before an unnamed threat. The ruin would become a tomb, an empire of darkness drawing us inwards, an ominous reminder of our mortality. Exploring underground ruins, one of the Abbé Prévost's heroes comes upon decomposed human remains; beside them lies a casket on which is written: *Furori sacrum*. The casket contains a weapon. Fury hovers in the heart of the ruins, and old unexpiated crimes threaten to recoil upon our own destiny. In the eighteenth century human sensitivity was not averse to the macabre effects of darkness among the ruins. For minds uncertain of their relationship with their own past, with their own history, the ambiguity adopted an imaginative background in which there loomed a ghostly avenger. In the lyricism of the "poetry of tombs" old fearful superstitions may be perpetuated.

The Gothic arch, before it was rediscovered by historians and experts, was the chosen background of solemnity on which to conjure up the spectacle of an anguished ritual, in which profanation alternated with punishment. At the beginning of Horace Walpole's *Castle of Otranto* a gigantic helmet falls from the sky, to crush the remote descendant of a usurper: the son pays for the crimes of his father and his forbears. It is as though this modest respectable gentleman, with his intellectual freedom, had wished to evade the dullness of an uneventful life by creating a universe overflowing with guilt and affliction. In order to nourish his Gothic dream he had constructed an appropriate setting on his property at Strawberry Hill. It seems likely, as Sir Kenneth Clark has suggested, that this setting corresponded to a sentimental vision of himself as a hero: to live in a Gothic setting is to live in a legend, to encircle the boredom of life, as with a protective ring or a halo, by an intense dreamworld freely inhabited by the phantasmas of violence, incest and catastrophe. Thus a wealthy polite bachelor was inflicting on himself the torments of a villainous tyrant. "With the help of a crumbling arch, the admirer of *Night Thoughts* could contemplate himself as a work of art" (Sir Kenneth Clark). These were "pleasures of the imagination," introducing a shudder of fear into a life which was to all appearances calm and flat. They were "artificial" emotions which reached their paroxysm all the more surely for taking place in an imaginary setting, in the internal musings of the imagination, without seeking any extension into real life. It was this illusionism that Jane Austen, while herself perhaps captivated to some extent by the "Gothic" imagination, satirized charmingly in *Northanger Abbey*.

This macabre pleasure adopted an archaic background to mark the discrepancy between the ideals of the imagination and the disappointments of present reality, and to regain contact with a "primitive" world in which man was still capable of high passion. When eighteenth-century man wearied of seeking out live sensations in a rapid succession of discontinuous instants, he finally turned towards an image of past greatness. His motive is clear: these primitive worlds (whether they were exotic, Hellenic, Gothic, Ossianic) were lost paradises of energy and intensity. To return, in the imagination, to a heroic past is equivalent to a pretense of sensory rejuvenation. This involved a revaluation of the "barbarous." "Poetry," wrote Diderot, "demands something tremendous, barbarous, savage." The Gothic, which had long been judged barbarous, was now to be considered *poetic*. We may venture to affirm that terror itself, for this sensibility in search of stimulation, came to be yearned for nostalgically. The myths of guilt, placed in an archaic setting, were to exercise a fascination similar to that of the ocean, forest, mountain or storm. The mind sought refuge in a perilous sublimity, in a fearful experience, simultaneously natural and religious, a center of irresistible energy which would recharge the bodily machine.

In the event, as from the late seventeenth century, the most constant interpretation of the Gothic style suggested that its origins were in nature: its form was taken from forest or rock. Certain Gothic buildings, according to Félibien, "have retained some of the rusticity of the lairs or caves in which the northern peoples used to live; the others have something of the lightness of the leafy arbors which one comes across in woods, or which the peoples in temperate climates construct to provide shade in open country." In these buildings there are "very slender columns... like so many branches or trunks of trees." A man enters a Gothic cathedral with the feeling that he is going into a forest. As opposed to Laugier, who saw the origin of architecture in the pillar, the young Goethe, in 1772, praised the pointed arch: the basic invention consisted of "two poles crossing at their tips, two more further back, and one placed lengthwise across the top, to form the ridge." He considered that it was both nature and genius that inspired in the designer of Strasbourg cathedral the means of diversifying the immense wall by sending it skywards "like a majestic tree of God, spreading wide, with thousands of branches, millions of boughs, and leaves as numerous as grains of sand by the sea, proclaiming to all the surrounding countryside the splendor of God, his Master." It is clear that the "Gothic" sensibility of the young Goethe, far from giving in to the fascination of the obscure, was in sympathy with a deep-rooted vital energy now soaring victoriously into the heights. This return to the Gothic was therefore the return to a source, and more than this, to a national source —Gallic or Nordic—to which certain minds thought they were more naturally bound, more profoundly related, than to the grace of porticoes and colonnades.

It was at this period that throughout most of Europe the idyll was medievalized, decked out in the array of courtly chivalry or of "troubadourism." This movement was encouraged also by other factors. In France the "nobiliary reaction" wished to remove the abuses of absolutism by reinstating the council of nobles to the functions which it had held in the early Middle Ages: originally the monarch—according to Boulainvilliers or Montesquieu—was simply a chief elected by his peers, *primus inter pares*. Among the lesser nobility, who provided so many writers up to the time of Romanticism, medievalism was not only an ideological weapon against the "tyranny" of the absolute monarchy, it was equally a battle refrain against the propaganda of the Encyclopaedists. The idyllic and mystical images of the Middle Ages elaborated in certain milieux (as expounded for example in Chateaubriand's *Génie du Christianisme*) tended to transfer into the past history of the nation and into the order of the Christian faith those values of plenitude that the humanist tradition had constantly situated in Greek and Roman antiquity.

Timidly and slowly, men were moving away from the image of the Middle Ages treated as a *capriccio* by Ariosto or rendered in a Baroque style by Tasso. To meet the sentimental needs of the century, they began to imagine a kind of golden age of the faith, in which the union of hearts and fusion with nature were thought to have taken the supreme form of communion in God. It was for Romanticism to complete the myth of the "organic" plenitude of medieval Christianity. But, here and there—in its combination of dissatisfaction, erudition and dreams —the eighteenth century was itself preparing the way for these conversions, by the aesthetic which held that irrational emotion before the beauty of religious worship and the solemnity of tradition counted for more than any *reasons* for believing. Skeptical and disillusioned minds cultivated the faith as a form of nostalgia, nourished and maintained by collections of touching pictures of bygone ages. This was fruitful ground also for illuminati and visionaries: adepts gathered around Cagliostro, Swedenborg, Mesmer, Martinez, Saint-Martin, at precisely the time when scientists were being influenced by the sober astronomical mechanics of Laplace. Such is the difficulty experienced by certain minds in giving up the idea of a supernaturally animated universe: if the terrestrial world precludes the consummation of the idyll, they must seek communion with the angels!

THE FASCINATION OF TERROR

Ossian and Shakespeare presented an opportunity for reviving history painting. They provided artists with dramatic situations of extraordinary grandeur, which caused the imagination to dismiss the traditional figures of antiquity and turn instead to the subjects of Celtic or medieval legend. This development was not always easy: the eclectic painters, attached to the Academic ideal, continued to hold Guido Reni and Michelangelo in absolute veneration. The story of Miravan, as depicted by Wright, is set in a Neoclassical crypt; the hero's clothes are an odd combination of folding Roman robes and an Oriental headdress. The general theme is the macabre representation of an act of desecration and an ancestral curse, the violation of a taboo and an offense against the Father: these elements of the picture reveal the spirit of the age. But the disparity, the discordance between the style and the theme is, in fact, involuntarily effective in the somber half-light of Wright's chiaroscuro.

Boydell, the wealthy London publisher, commissioned the best artists of the age to illustrate a new edition of Shakespeare's works. The Shakespeare Gallery *marks a date in the history of European sensibility. The scenes from Shakespeare which most usually caught the attention of the English painters of the second half of the century were those in which man confronted mysterious forces transcending his own nature: storms, witches, ghosts. Under the supernatural threat of an enraged universe the individual's reaction was spontaneous and defiant. In a gesture of lyrical intensity man created an image of his own greatness in function of the magnitude of the perils he had to overcome.*

Classical taste considered that this was an immoderate, frenzied barbarousness. But the barbarous was very soon to be regarded as an essential attribute of the sublime—so much so, in fact, that Homer and the Greek tragic poets retained their prestige only because the new sensibility saw in them, not order and balance, but the savage poetry of man's turbulent origins.

JOSEPH WRIGHT, CALLED WRIGHT OF DERBY (1734-1797). MIRAVAN BREAKING OPEN THE TOMBS OF HIS ANCESTORS, 1772. COURTESY OF DERBY ART GALLERY COMMITTEE.

JOHN RUNCIMAN (1744-1768). KING LEAR, 1767. THE NATIONAL GALLERIES OF SCOTLAND, EDINBURGH.

GEORGE ROMNEY (1734-1802). THE TEMPEST. GALLERIA NAZIONALE D'ARTE MODERNA, ROME.

THE ASSEMBLED UNIVERSE

The Abbé Du Bos, at the beginning of the century, affirmed that "at present our painters are acquainted with a nature of trees and animals more beautiful and more perfect than the nature known to the precursors of Raphael." The idyll was impossible and yet nature remained ever present. But one form of art did succeed in bringing out both the presence and the impossibility: landscape gardening. The superior function of this art, to some observers, was that it apparently achieved the perfect reconciliation of nature and culture. Its aim was to have human labors encourage perfection in nature, instead of wrongly conflicting with it—to return to the original paradise of wild nature, without however giving up the slowly acquired attributes of science and reflection; so that man's powers of reason, instead of separating him *from* nature, would actually bring him back more readily into contact *with* nature. This was the role of the Elysium set up by the heroine of Rousseau's *Nouvelle Héloïse*: the reinstatement of primitive happiness through a perfection of art, an organized festival of natural plantlife, the symbolic counterpart of the political *Contrat Social*.

This particular vision of nature, cultivated in such a way as to efface all traces of human intervention, was not exactly the same as that which constituted the setting for the naive idyll of the beginnings of time, experienced with unthinking spontaneity. It was now a conscious *return*, in which the mind successfully perfected its development by a full awareness of having gone back to its beginnings. It was not the unity that preceded separation and nostalgia; it was the union of what had been divided, of what had been compelled to undergo dispersal and exile. It then remained only to secure the harmony of "les belles âmes," their victory over the divisions which had gradually been introduced by the evil of society. This would be the recovery of plenitude; but, instead of the original *innocence*, unaware of good and evil, it would initiate the reign of *virtue*, victorious over evil, and rich from its experience of anxiety. Similarly the "social

contract" replaced the anarchical *independence* of man's origins by a *liberty* accepted consciously by enlightened minds.

This "romantic" dream, which was to inspire so many "landscape gardens," was itself only the expression (expanded to the dimension of a Neoplatonic metaphysics of the return to the One) of a revolution which had taken place in the design of gardens. Abandoning its taste for the geometrically ordered gardens perfected by Le Nôtre, the cultured public of the eighteenth century, first in England, then in France, had become wildly enthusiastic about hilly parks, with winding footpaths and irregularly scattered clumps of trees with freely spreading foliage, giving the impression of a completely untamed nature. This search for variety, irregularity, sinuosity has been compared to certain characteristics of the Rococo style. But, more deeply, A.O. Lovejoy has shown that the fashion for the "jardin anglais" corresponded to a profound transformation in man's idea of nature. The original idea had been that a geometer-God (or geometer-nature) always organized creation on the simplest lines, the basic primitive operations forming straight lines or perfect circles; consequently geometric beauty, clearly intelligible, had been regarded as natural beauty. To explain the irregularity, the asymmetry of natural objects, it had been necessary to point out contingent obstacles, the inertia of material reality. Thus by geometrizing nature, trimming shrubbery, laying perfectly straight footpaths, man was creating a purified image of nature, reinstating the basic natural forms. Now, however, as a result of philosophical reflection and a whole series of aesthetic experiences (including the discovery of Chinese garden design), men were increasingly convinced that variety, wildness and apparent disorder were the normal state of nature, and that, as a result, man's intervention with tape and clippers was contrary to the free growth and development of natural forms. Once again the notion of *obstacle* was introduced, but now it was in order to incriminate man's "corrective" efforts and not as an objection to the strange, complex, irregular products everywhere visible in the physical world. The image of nature which then became current was more obscure, charged with irrationality: it was a triumph of energy, not in geometrical figures, but in the whim of organic creation. This is the lesson discernable in the gardens designed by Alexander Pope, William Kent or William Chambers. At the period when industry was beginning to disfigure the English towns and countryside, paradisiacal reserves were created for those who intended to enjoy the profits of industry (or their revenue from plantations worked by Negro slaves) without sacrificing the contemplation of untouched nature.

This is perhaps the secret reason why the regained idyll of Clarens remained a romantic dream, and also why the superb landscape gardens of the late eighteenth century looked rather like cemeteries. The privileged place was in a way haunted by the vague awareness that it was *preserved*, a sanctuary: it was, in fact, merely an *asylum*. Watelet commented as follows: "When an ingenious, sensitive man whose time is his own has organized the wealth and beauty of nature according to his own tastes, he naturally holds these new treasures in particular affection. So, to guarantee his own private, untroubled enjoyment of the garden, he digs ditches around it and erects fences and walls: he constructs an enclosure. The garden is then an emblem of his own personality, it is the tiny empire of the man who cannot increase his powers without increasing the accompanying cares and anxieties." While the storms of history were threatening outside, men gave themselves the illusion of living a moment of eternity. They seem to have wished that not only nature but the whole universe could be present in this garden, with distant places and monuments of the past brought together into their own lives, as a miniature representation of the whole of time and space. In his study on *Les Jardins et Pays d'illusion*, J. Baltrusaitis writes: "When the whole world is regarded as a garden, a garden may contain the world." A garden was therefore a microcosm containing the whole earth, in which one would if necessary be willing to shut oneself away permanently, since all places, all ages, and all forms of architecture could be embraced in a single nonchalant stroll. Exoticism was there, tamed and acclimatized. Rousseau describes Cobham's park

as follows: "The master and creator of this superb retreat has even had ruins, temples and old edifices built there: time and place are brought together in a superhuman spectacle of magnificence." So, beside the waterfalls, islands and artificial rocks, there were pagodas, Hindu temples, Greek ruins and Gothic chapels. General Conway had a replica of Palmyra erected in his gardens. Adorned with these artificial "fabrics", parks became open-air equivalents of private curio collections. In such gardens the taste for making collections could be indulged freely.

But collections of curios were not meant for idle daydreaming, whereas everything in these gardens was arranged to provoke reverie: pauses beside the water, viewpoints on some fictitious tomb, sights of "picturesque" horror, groves designed for the voluptuary. Through the skill of the landscape designer, the sensations would vary with the windings of the paths. For the garden was not to be simply a universe in miniature; it had also to be a material extension of the human psyche, in which all ages of life, and all the states of the soul (including other states than those found on the Carte du Tendre) could be scattered about the park and expressed in full by the variations of water and rock, of greenery and artificial or sculptured stone. It would be unjust to wax ironical about these designs, condemning them as falsifications, necessarily based on deception. A garden was primarily a work of art on an unaccustomed scale, a dream in which the dreamer walked with open eyes. "The form of nature rediscovered in gardens," writes Baltrusaitis, "was not that of a country 'meadow' extending behind a house: it was an evocation, a dream, an artifice." Further, the dream could only develop if the observer himself were to move along, with uneven rhythm and frequent pauses, as if led on by some kind of music. Thus the audience at the *Marriage of Figaro* were enraptured that the final scene should take place beneath the great chestnut-trees of a nocturnal park.

But in these retreats which were intended to gather everything into one place it is evident that "everything" was less present than represented; more, everything was less represented than recalled. The garden was a country of the memory. Most of its fabrics were, in one way or another, memorials: of love, virtue, philosophy. To this end the monuments were covered with inscriptions, with lines of verse: their architecture was eloquent, indeed it was garrulous. It perpetuated beloved features or glorious names. It would perhaps be more accurate to say that it introduced the *absence* of persons and places, the better to evoke their memory fervently, or to indulge in regret and gentle melancholy. It cultivated absence, or, in the artificial tombs, a pretense of absence: in this it was a double absence. The garden, instead of being a throbbing center of presence regained, was a meeting place for nostalgic anxiety. Even if they were not tombs, the fabrics were the phantasmal doubles of a distant reality. They were a pretense in which man could still sense the functional *image*. At the end of the poem *Jardins*, Jacques Delille was remaining faithful to the affective values bound up with his theme when he evoked a hero turning towards the vestiges of a bygone age and adoring the image of a happiness which was now beyond his grasp. Consequently the action of the garden on man's imagination was to deprive the immediate historical present of its special urgency. The eternal moment, in the labyrinth of false ruins, proclaimed the transience of greatness, the finality of death, the vanity of all things—with the single exception of the sentient mind which observed these things with a confused exaltation.

So, in the leafy shade, in spite of the hamlets and the dairies, in the heart of the gardens in which he sought the simple life, straining after the bucolic sound of cowbells, man's search for the idyll led only to an encounter with death. Yet again an illusory spectacle had been recomposed around the "sensitive souls" who had sought a living presence in the bosom of nature. What is to become of genuine feeling when man takes nature itself as his accomplice in a deliberate delusion which weakens his consciousness of reality and has him floundering in the imaginary?

7

THE DREAMWORLD OF
THE MIND

In Piranesi's *Carceri d'invenzione* the architectural "caprice" attained a great height of mystery and the magnitude of the masterpiece. From his early youth Piranesi combined an obsession with death with a delight in inventing extraordinary buildings. In some of his first engravings (which are actually small-scale "caprices") the idea of death is rendered by skulls, bones and clepsydras scattered among fallen bas-reliefs. His remarkable series of *Prisons*, the first of which date back earlier than 1750, was a source of inspiration to the Romantic poets (De Quincey, Gautier, Victor Hugo). The *Prisons* perhaps reveal something of Piranesi's personality. For example, Henri Focillon writes: "If, after constructing porticoes, temples, tombs and imaginary Capitols with such apparent indifference, he turned to prisons and lavished so much energy and such a wealth of fantasy on them, the origin of this preoccupation must surely lie in the most secret places of his heart, in the combination of melancholy and enthusiasm which marks his own private life and is also discernible in many of his works. From his imaginary prisons to his scenes of ruins and tombs, no matter how bright the shafts of sunlight are, and despite the beauty of the natural setting, we can sense the sadness latent in Piranesi's visionary soul. His sadness never leaves him as he makes his way among the relics of the past or when, with a strange premonition of the future, he erects the metallic buildings of a later age upon Etruscan *Cloacae* or on the grim *gemoniae* of Tiberius." In the *Prisons* we see a grandiose display of man's architectural genius, but these monuments are designed to abase and crush him. Are we being invited to share the merciless exaltation of an architect-executioner or the anguish of the fore-doomed prisoner? Piranesi's representations of prisons suggest a feeling diametrically opposed to the feeling evoked when he depicts ruins: it is a sense not of *having* forgotten but of *being* forgotten. While ruins suggest a keen observer idly reflecting on the unattainable secrets of the fallen stones, the *Prisons* suggest a dreamworld, a nightmare building whose countless vaults and spiral stairways remind the prisoner that he is forgotten forever, eternally cut off from human intercourse. The eighteenth century, which was to stress the dignity of human freedom, began with a keen awareness of the horror of the dungeon. This became almost an obsession: for example, in Sade's descriptions of dungeons, in which a secret "sect" delighted in vicious perversions; in true or fictitious tales about prisons; or in plays denouncing the arbitrary brutalities of the Inquisition and absolutism. Throughout the century the prison was a constant theme, sometimes as the background, sometimes as the characters' central experience. So when the French Revolution began with the destruction of the prison of the Bastille, this action was undoubtedly the result of an aversion profoundly rooted in the collective consciousness of France.

With his prolific imagination, Piranesi demonstrated a rare creative freedom in his representations of the restriction of human freedom. In Gothic settings the imagination voluntarily accepted physical limitations. While Gothic architecture was certainly admired, at one stage, for its lightness and whimsicality (as in Galliari's charming scenes), the tendency quickly arose to associate pointed arches with the experience of human anxiety and mortality. Thus Bentley's illustration for Gray's *Elegy* is based on Poussin's *Shepherds in Arcady*, but now seen through a Gothic archway. The theme of the churchyard (particularly the country churchyard) developed in European civilization at precisely the time when Piranesi was creating his *Prisons* and *Ruins*. It carried the same associations: the same evocation of the impossibility of recapturing past time, the same vain effort of the memory to overcome oblivion. But when William Beckford, after a long period in Portugal, returned to England and had Wyatt build the slender and delicate tower of Fonthill Abbey, it was in order to give his retreat a setting at once legendary and gigantic, so that he could live a life of constant exaltation. And from the strange Oriental tale of *Vathek* we learn that the vertical soaring movement of the pseudo-Gothic Fonthill Abbey was intended not as an act of devotion but of blasphemy; he used religious architecture as an act of defiance against God.

This was the point at which attitudes and sentiments were being reversed, when the sense of man's weakness, of his inefficacity before the universe was being converted into a spirit of power and domination. Boullée, Ledoux and the other architects of the late eighteenth century who sought to give their creations significant, "eloquent" forms, brushed aside metaphysical obstructions such as the sense of guilt or the imminence of death and allowed imagination free rein. Boullée's cenotaph rises triumphantly: death itself becomes a living force. Ledoux likened himself quite frankly to the Demiurge, seeing the architect as "a Titan of the Earth, a rival of the god who created the globe." Like Goethe's Faust he proudly declared: "I shall move mountains and drain the fens dry." Although he built elaborate mansions for the actresses and wealthy upstarts of Louis XVI's reign, Boullée became a sort of Demiurge when working on plans for futuristic buildings governed by simplicity of geometrical form. The circle and the sphere, as he used them, no longer symbolized the perfection of the physical world. Copernicus and Galileo had triumphed, the earth was no longer regarded as the center of the universe and space was now considered to be infinite. But man, on the other hand, had become the central point of a sphere over which he had absolute control. His central position is skillfully suggested by Ledoux's sketch of the pupil of an eye reflecting the rising tiers of the circular theater at Besançon: through this image man is symbolized at once as creator, actor and spectator.

THE DREAMWORLD OF THE MIND

1. Giambattista Piranesi (1720-1778): Plate 7 of the *Prisons* (first state), second edition, about 1761. Etching.

2. Richard Bentley (1708-1782): Frontispiece for Thomas Gray's *Elegy Written in a Country Churchyard*, 1751. Engraving.

3. Fabrizio Galliari (1709-1790): Gothic Atrium, before 1765-1767. Drawing.

4. James Wyatt (1747-1813): The Octagon of Fonthill Abbey, 1795-1807. Engraving from John Britton's *Illustrations of Fonthill Abbey*, 1823.

5. Claude-Nicolas Ledoux (1736-1806): Design for a Shelter for the Rural Guards. Engraving.

6. Pierre-Jules Delépine (1756-1835): Design for a Monument in Honor of Newton. Engraving.

7. Etienne-Louis Boullée (1728-1799): Design for a Cenotaph. Engraving.

8. Claude-Nicolas Ledoux (1736-1806): Perspective View of the Town of Chaux, second project. Engraving.

9. Claude-Nicolas Ledoux (1736-1806): Symbolic Presentation of the Theater of Besançon through the Pupil of an Eye. Engraving.

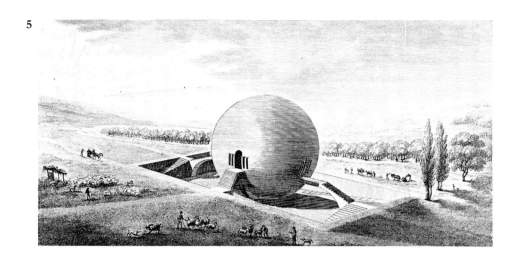

5

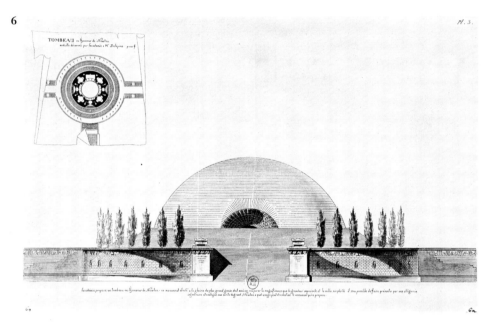

6

7

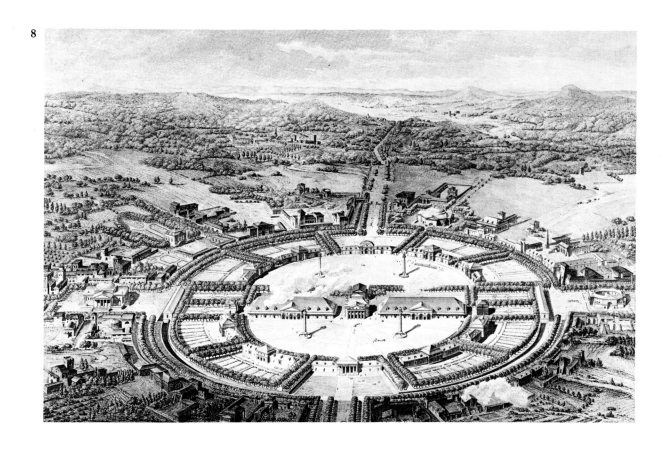

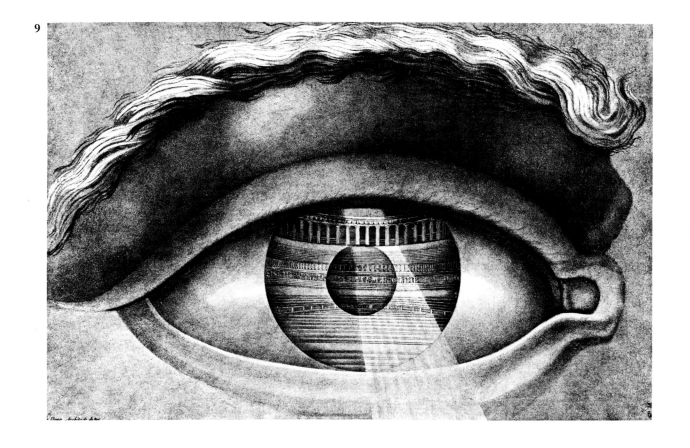

THE STYLE OF WILLPOWER

So man mused nostalgically in the gardens, and his aspiration towards the idyll left him longing for an elusive harmony. He was experiencing a singular joy, which consisted of an exquisite sense of the absence of joy.

But while landscape gardens allowed nature to develop erratically, in apparent disorder, Neoclassical façades, corresponding to these gardens, were remarkable for their simplicity, their geometrical nudity, their absence of ornamentation. It is as though, by the end of the eighteenth century, the formal relationship between houses and gardens had been shifted and reversed: Baroque façades, decorative, organic, alive, had overlooked geometrically planned gardens: Neoclassical buildings, in which (as Emil Kaufmann has shown) the concatenations and gradations were replaced by geometrical segmentation, overlooked parks in which the organic power of nature was given free play. It would seem that the traditional requirement of order and variety, being perhaps unable to achieve a universal *fusion* of these two qualities, was expressed instead in a balanced *opposition*. Provided that the opposition was maintained and that the various tensions were counterbalanced, this constituted a structural system fulfilling the norms of aesthetic coherence. Though differently distributed, the sum total of energy in the system remained constant.

But in this particular case the modification was of particular consequence. The Baroque system had operated a kind of double intersection. It had often contrasted with rationalized gardens building-façades decorated with plant motifs. The reign of man and the reign of nature had certainly remained distinct but they had exchanged their characteristics, merging into each other for the sake of ornamentation and prestige. On the other hand, the "English style" park, in which man's intervention was supposed to remain invisible, was intended to offer the majestic spectacle of the wishes, the *purposefulness* of nature;

while within, but separate from the actual park, the houses constructed by Morris or Adam manifested the *will* of man, isolating clearly the presence of human reason in the midst of the irrational domains of freely growing vegetation. The Baroque interpretation of man and nature was now replaced by a separation, thus establishing the distance between man and nature which was a prerequisite for nostalgic contemplation. Now, as we have seen, this contemplative separation arose as a compensatory or expiatory reaction against the growing attitude of practical men towards nature. While technical exploitation tended to wage war on nature, houses and parks attempted a reconciliation, a local armistice, introducing the dream of an impossible peace: and to this end men had continued to retain the image of untouched natural surroundings.

The constructions, and even more the plans, of Boullée, Ledoux, or Poyet, are striking for their monumental proportions, their vigor, their impressive use of simple mass. They manifested a new eloquence (which was probably to some extent indebted to the majesty of Rome, to Seneca and the Sant'Angelo tower). As opposed to the eloquence of the Baroque, the effect sought after was not movement and profusion, but an elemental force whose energy would appear controlled and static. We are in the presence of a sense of purpose which has voluntarily renounced its normal external characteristics and turned itself purely into *mass*. The aesthetic of the grand décor has been replaced by an aesthetic of restrained sublimity. In this way man's Promethean willpower could counterbalance nature's "titanic" strength. In searching for what Quatremère de Quincy called a "standard of imitation" in nature, man invented a *style of strength* to stand in contrast to the strength of nature. Nature was infinite, but there was, according to Burke, an artificial infinite which consisted of "a uniform succession of great parts." Moreover, this willpower was not simply concentrated in an impressive simplicity of form;

it was perceptible in the tendency to show clearly the purpose of particular buildings, by symbolizing distinctly their *finality*. This constituted the growth of what Georges Cattaui has called "architectural symbolics"—the most perfect example being Boullée's plan for the Cenotaph for Newton. If in this instance one can speak of expressive finality, other works can be said to show a functional finality (using the term *functional* in its most modern sense): libraries, hospitals, prisons, tenements were so conceived that their structure had the double attribute of indicating and complying strictly with their function.

Strength and finality: these two aspects of architectural *intentionality*—or *volontarisme*—corresponded to a growing intellectual and moral current at the end of the eighteenth century. It is remarkable that this functional intentionality should have been contemporary with the taste for ruins and funereal reverie. Did the ideal dreamers and the purposeful minds belong to different social groups? This could appear to be so if we indulged hastily in the tendency to explain states of mind in sociological terms—nostalgia pertaining to the declining class, that is, to the nobility, and triumphant energy being an attribute of the young bourgeois eager to possess a world worthy of their desires. On closer examination, however, we find that long episodes of "melancholy" or "spleen" characterized the opening stages of certain triumphantly willful careers. Does this mean that "Wertherism" was an affectation, an artificial pose dictated by fashion, which the young bourgeois discarded as soon as they knew themselves better? I would prefer to believe that as far as Goethe, Chateaubriand, Alfieri and Maine de Biran were concerned, they underwent a fundamental experience in which liberty found its initial outlet in an act of nostalgic non-compliance, in a purposeless desire. Discovering the world and other people wanting and unable to offer the idyllic plenitude that would have made happiness possible, the disconsolate mind, haunted by a sense of lack, found that it knew nothing beyond itself and came to recognize itself in everything; but by the same token it realized its power to create a *universe of sensibility*. In dreaming of a past age or of a spatial distance which it could not attain, the imagination found that it was itself a creative power. Beginning with Rousseau the century saw the growth of sentimental *solitude*: a solitude in which man both suffered from his separation and enjoyed a purposeless freedom which was, so to speak, expended

within itself. The energy of desire and of hopeless nostalgia was used up within the plane of the self. Lacking any application in the external world, this unrelieved energy could recoil against the individual himself: whence the suicide of Werther, and inclination towards suicide in Goethe and Chateaubriand. But, as we well know, and as so many works of the imagination testify, this energy can find an outlet—while still maintaining its distance from "concrete" reality—in the elaboration of imaginary objects: poems, works of art. *Narrate* the desire and the nostalgia; write a story about the suicide or the mortal sorrow, so that they may be defined and exorcised. By this means, by this experience, through the secondary life which is art, the creative will transmutes the destructive forces from which it has suffered so intensely. So it is as though many adolescents in the late eighteenth century underwent an experience of melancholy which, while glorifying a belief in "liberty for death," made this same liberty serviceable, mobilizing it with a view to artistic creation or to a revolt against "tyranny" *(Sturm und Drang)*. The purposefulness underlying non-compliance was consequently used to offset the temptation towards deliberate self-destruction which continually haunted the experience of melancholy. From this time onwards man was bound to be aware that he was willpower and that he lived by willpower.

But this purposeful liberty was not to be applied only to the elaboration of works of art. Balzac was not wrong to interpret the career of Napoleon as an adventure of the will. And it is no surprise to find that the speculation of certain occultists held that acts of the will were identical with the fulgurations of the electric fluid. For Mesmer and his adepts, the "animal magnetism" developed by the will of the magnetizer was much more efficacious than the power of a magnet. "A man has the ability to exercise a salutary influence on other men by directing upon them, by his willpower, the principle which animates us and gives us life... Therefore, to magnetize, the first condition is to will" (Deleuze). Gnostics and theosophists revived the old theories of the practical efficacy of the imagination.

Thus the eighteenth century, which had opened with the predominance of a philosophy in which subjectivity was defined principally by sensation, closed upon a philosophy according to which subjectivity was defined essentially by willpower: by spontaneous liberty (Kant), by effort (Maine de Biran). Intent originally on sensation, men had found life in a discontinuous succession of sensory enjoyments; this style of life had consisted of a series of dissimilar instants, which had in fact to be as dissimilar as possible in order to renew one's surprise and avoid the boredom of repetition. Such lives had no distant goal, no finality beyond the limits of the imminent moment of time. As Georges Poulet has shown, life had passively assumed the form of the sinuous line, manifesting "a tireless ability to comply with the dictates of chance," and degenerating finally into "complete aimlessness." But this episodic style made up of chance events and momentary excesses, was replaced by a *style of willpower* or *purpose*, in which life was organized, given precise ends, "finalized." The century therefore seems to have evolved from the subjectivity of sensation to the subjectivity of will. This is borne out by the architecture of Boullée and Ledoux, as well as by the *Liaisons Dangereuses*, the *Magic Flute* and Beethoven's symphonies; nor should we forget the triumphs of willpower made possible by the Revolution and the Empire. The breach was opening and human energies were at last to find their application in the social sphere, in "concrete" reality, in a universe to be invaded and subjugated.

The old doctrines of willpower undoubtedly played their part: stoicism, Plutarch, Descartes, the Jesuits... Only what was developing in the late eighteenth century was a Promethean *volontarisme*, intent on dominating nature and controlling history. Man's willpower created a new spatio-temporal universe in which to develop and assume material form. The co-ordinates within which the mind had henceforth resolved to act were Nature and Time. By comparison, we could affirm that the *volontarisme* of the Renaissance or the Baroque period constituted nothing more than a search for the illustrious stability of rational man, upon a background of extratemporal, eternal values. Instead of being defined as an evolving power, the human will saw itself as a power of obstruction, of resistance to universal "change" and the fluidity of appearances. At its extreme limit, the ostentatious display of willpower became an end in itself. How should we explain the difference in style between the "old" *volontarisme* and that of the late eighteenth century? The great change seems to me to be closely associated with a transformation in that image of the world which informs the particular characteristics of man's will-

power. Until the seventeenth century, the idea of destiny, of a universal chain of cause and effect, of physical necessity, had been the consequence of man's sensory experience, and had found its extension in speculative systems on the lines of astrology. The human will, if it wished to defy the fates, had little hold over the physical world, so its only resource was steadfast resolution and contempt for the assaults from without. After Bacon, Galileo, Descartes and Newton, the eighteenth century discovered that physical necessity could be defined in terms of *natural laws*, that these laws could be formulated in the language of mathematics, and that through these laws man's thought could grasp, if not the quality of the external world, at least its definable phenomena. One of the first conclusions that the eighteenth century drew from the discovery that nature was governed by mechanical laws, was certainly that man himself was conditioned by these laws. But if man was a being determined by nature, he was determined in such a way that he could acquire, through knowledge, the means of intervening, in his turn, in the natural course of cause and effect; he could modify himself, educate or corrupt himself; he could change the face of the world; and he could carry out his enterprises the more successfully for respecting the natural law and using it faithfully as the instrument of his own wishes.

These views determined the range of possibilities for a technical expansion of the human will. It was now possible to go beyond the ancient "self-mastery" and aim at mastery of the world. Thus man, having understood the natural law and having, in the act of acquiring this knowledge, realized the fundamental basis of his freedom, was to be able to throw himself wholeheartedly into works of creation or of transformation. The future was opening on new works of art, on new utilitarian undertakings, on the great reforms of human society. Steam engines, mechanical looms, ideal cities or new dramaturgies.

In Goya's phrase, when the reason slumbers, its dreams engender monsters. The glorious dreams which began with a sketchy knowledge of the laws of nature invited men, by turns, to reproduce the origin of life and to predict the end of time, to create artificially the first stirrings of life, or to draw up plans for man's future happiness: anthropogeny and Utopianism.

Do robots belong to the history of art or to technical history? Their creators wish to imitate the organic finality of life, by a curious combination of the perfection, the finality of the mechanical instrument and the "eternal finality" of the plaything. If we suppose that nature acts on the model of man's machines, what is there to prevent us dreaming up a machine so perfect that it would do almost anything that nature is capable of? Could man's rational calculations not introduce the movements of life into inanimate matter? In 1738, Vaucanson had presented his mechanical duck: "an artificial duck, of gilded copper, which eats, drinks, quacks, dabbles about in water, and digests food like a living duck." Jaquet-Droz, with his *androids* and his charming *Lady Musician* (1773) who could play five tunes, and curtsy and breathe, most certainly imparted the highest opinion of man's powers of mechanical invention. At the period when God was being praised as the great clock-maker, why should some human clock-maker not become a little god? But the demonstration was ambiguous. After the first moment of surprise, everyone could see that the gestures were stereotyped, that the repertoire included nothing unforeseen or accidental, and that the smiles lacked all human gradation. The poets then took to creating the fanciful nightmare of a woman, surpassing all other women, a delightful creature you would like to clasp in your arms— which was in fact only a great toy, worked by cams, cylinders and bellows. After Lavoisier and Priestley the dreamers turned away from mechanical contrivances to the new experiments in chemistry in order to further the great study of the *homunculus* which had so fascinated the alchemists. In Goethe we find two versions of the myth: he had related the story of an automaton, a robot, which was passionately loved, while in *Faust* he presented the development, *in vitro*, of a little test-tube man. Could the chemist not be nature's equal if he succeeded in sharing with her the secret of man's origins?

But the "Faustian" ambition *par excellence* is the material transformation of the world and the founding of an order of reason within both human society and physical space.

The century had seen an abundance of "true systems," sometimes under the appearance of prophecies or imaginary journeys: "natural codes," vindications of rights, projects, and wild fancies.

In all this the history of today can see an involved tangle of calculations of abstract reason, barely disguised projects of longing reverie, naive simplifications and, very often, a reversed nostalgia, directed towards the future instead of looking back towards the golden age or the primitive idyll. These notions all fermented and brought results, confirming Leibnitz's affirmation that "thought tends to action." To imagine an *ideal city* was no longer simply an abstract exercise in ingenuity, it was a concrete aim, a tension requiring practical relief, a mode of thought which estimated the conditions necessary for it to become reality. The historians of architecture have observed that it would be erroneous to dismiss the cities of Ledoux as Utopian: they were monumental *projects*, whose practicability had been considered lucidly by their creator. In his plans for the town of Chaux, Ledoux studied the relationship of the construction with the surrounding countryside, besides the various functions of the architectural space, and he finally proposed solutions which appear Utopian but which twentieth-century specialists nevertheless praise for their "modernity." When Sébastien Mercier imagined, for the year 2440, regulated traffic, fountains at every corner, lighted flights of steps, decent hospitals, a city with flat roofs, all the same height and converted into gardens, we must observe that his anticipatory description, which was in many respects very timid (he foresaw none of our scientific acquisitions), was guided less by an extravaganza of invention than by the desire to create something *desirable*. He was a perfecter rather than a perfectionist. The architects of the time, in England, France and Italy, were guided by the same ideal.

Having thus discovered its own efficacity, in the perspective of a past interpreted as a long progress, and a present considered to be modifiable, man's willpower adopted the future as its special dimension. Its great themes were: construct, discover, perfect.

At the beginning of the century, as we have seen, man lived, as it were, with the sinuous line, his life consisting of a sequence of dissimilar sensations, an alternation of physical pleasure and abstract reflection, a discontinuous series of temptations, enjoyments and surprises. Then, towards the last third of the century, a change began to take place, and life centered around the energetic pursuit of given ends. The same transformation took place in man's image of the history of humanity. An early generation of eighteenth-century thinkers had repudiated the conception of divine intervention in history, with Providence achieving ends invisible to man; this they replaced by an interpretation of history as a series of *vicissitudes*, developing in an alternation of *corsi e ricorsi* (Vico), of moments of greatness and of decadence, fluctuating between civilization and barbarism. Then, in the closing decades of the century, the image of history as a finalized progression was reinstated, with its finality now postulated, not by the will of God, but by the common will of mankind. This new vision conceived history as governed by an immanent tension which nineteenth-century philosophy was to define as a "gradual growth of the mind," and which the theorists of progress, around 1789, called a "principle of advancement." The *Esquisse d'un tableau historique des progrès de l'esprit humain*, which Condorcet wrote shortly before his execution, ends with a tableau of the "future progress of the human mind." This man, whom the discords of the Revolution were to condemn to such a premature death, claimed that man's own *prevision* (or foresight) could supply a knowledge of the future which the theoretical tradition had attributed solely to the prospective insight of God, that is, to divine Providence. On the basis of his knowledge, man can foresee; on the basis of his foresight, he can act: "If man can predict with almost complete assurance the phenomena whose laws he knows, and if, even when he does not know them, he can use his experience of the past to foresee future events with great probability, why then should it be considered idle and illusory to draw up with some degree of verisimilitude an outline of the future destiny of mankind, on the basis of the results of history?... Our hopes for the future state of mankind can be reduced to three major points: the destruction of inequality between nations, the progress of equality within any one nation, and the real amelioration of man himself."

Are we to regard this simply as a scientific conjecture? There is a sense of man's eager flight towards the future, the feeling that man's willpower has conferred upon him, almost magically, a power of levitation. This hunted, imprisoned man escaped literally into a future dimension...

An eager flight! Must we consider it a mere coincidence that the old dream of flight began to reach fulfillment precisely at the end of the eighteenth century? For centuries Utopias had been discovered at the end of imaginary journeys by sea, or after fantastic flights. This tradition had been continued in the eighteenth century. Rousseau had dreamed of a "New Daedalus," Restif had sent a flying man to discover the austral lands, Nicholas Klim had glided down towards the center of the earth. The first aerostats demonstrated successfully the conquest of the vertical dimension so far forbidden to man. Worked by fire, and helped by the lightness of hydrogen, for all its dangers, this lifting power intoxicated the aeronauts and their ambition was to control and *steer* their great paper spheres, so capricious and unmanageable. Once the first intoxication of these haphazard flights was over, the two major desires were to establish *communications* between distant places and to carry out high-altitude *observations*: to *exchange* and to *know*. Ascension, the symbol of the liberated will, immediately aimed at the growth of scientific knowledge and the tightening of bonds between nations.

A magnificent picture by Guardi heralds, in the emblem of the aerostat, the accession of this *style of willpower*, seen from a shore seething with Rococo humanity, in masks and capes, intent on their pursuit of the scattered instants of pleasure. With melancholy circumspection the scene summarizes the century as a whole. Are these elegant men, so like agile insects, aware that this present sensation marks the end of their world, and that the sign in the sky, more than the comets of old, is prophesying an inexorable revolution? The little sphere hovering perilously in the blue distance is the hazardous form of the future. From above, what would one see? The question remains, literally, in suspense. But Guardi's painting, and the eighteenth-century observers whom it represents, now seem to be imprisoned in the past. The joy of perceiving and rendering candidly, naively, a fleeting instant of man's life was perhaps here for the last time. There followed the endless confrontation of man's willpower and infinity, the permanent injunction to go beyond present knowledge and achievements, the long evolution in which our own destinies are being enacted.

THE ART OF SEEING

"Our sight is the most perfect and most delightful of all our senses. It fills the mind with the largest variety of ideas, converses with objects at the greatest distance, and continues the longest in action without being tired or satiated with its proper enjoyments... Our sight... may be considered as a more delicate and diffusive sense of touch, that spreads itself over an infinite multitude of bodies, comprehends the largest figures, and brings into our reach some of the most remote parts of the universe"—Addison's words might have been written in front of some picture by Guardi showing a throng of people engrossed in the pleasures of the eye. Guardi is usually thought of as a painter of views, an artist forever under the spell of the light and space of Venice, the pink marble of San Marco and the gleaming waters of the lagoon. But Guardi was also a master of crowd scenes, which he reduced to a glittering mass of capes, masks and tricorns. He loved the colorful surge of the crowd as it gathered to watch some ceremony, pageant, or unusual event: the Doge's wedding of the sea, the reception of an ambassador, the Carnival, a ball, an opera, a fire. His Venetians seem in fact to have no occupation other than that of onlookers, delightedly absorbed in the immediate sights and scenes of the world around them.

Such was the century of the Enlightenment which looked at things in the clear sharp light of the reasoning mind whose processes appear to have been closely akin to those of the seeing eye. For sight is the most expansive of all our senses: a glance is the conquest of distance. And reason, in the eighteenth century, also carried man far, so far that he found the mere world of the senses insufficient. Reason sought truth beyond the veil of appearances; its aim was to anticipate the tangible instant. To aspire, to will, is to foresee—to see what is not yet visible or existent through what is visible or existent. Insight is foresight. When the style of willpower triumphed, things became means to an end and were no longer valued for their own sake. Fortunately for Guardi, he lived in an earlier day. But the time was coming when any artist who clung persistently and lovingly to the outward appearance of things would seem to be dallying over the frivolous pleasures of childhood.

FRANCESCO GUARDI (1712-1793). THE ASCENSION OF A BALLOON OVER THE GIUDECCA CANAL, VENICE.
GEMÄLDEGALERIE, STAATLICHE MUSEEN, BERLIN-DAHLEM.

LIST OF ILLUSTRATIONS

INDEX OF NAMES

SKIRA

TEXT AND COLOR PLATES PRINTED BY
IRL IMPRIMERIES RÉUNIES LAUSANNE S.A.

BINDING BY
H. + J. SCHUMACHER AG, SCHMITTEN (FRIBOURG)

PHOTOGRAPHS BY

Archives photographiques, Paris (page 125), Aerofilms & Aero Pictorial Ltd., London (page 47 below), Agraci, Paris (page 122 below), Alinari, Florence (page 35 upper left), Jean Arlaud, Geneva (page 152 lower left), Carlo Aschieri, Milan (page 201 below), Maurice Babey, Basel (pages 18, 19, 20, 21, 26, 29, 46 below, 48 above, 59, 61, 77, 78, 93, 97, 110 above, 129, 132, 138, 139, 143, 153, 193), Carlo Bevilacqua, Milan (pages 62, 141, 182), Henry B. Beville, Washington (pages 68, 96, 130, 144), Joachim Blauel, Munich (page 92), Paul Boissonnas, Geneva (pages 36 upper left, 106 below, 109 above, 155 upper left and below), Bulloz, Paris (pages 49 above, 152 lower right), Chomon-Perino, Turin (page 175 lower right), Focco, Madrid (page 24), John R. Freeman & Co, Ltd, London (page 165), Marc Garanger, Lyons (pages 170, 187), Giraudon, Paris (pages 109 below, 124 lower right), Hansa-Luftbild GMBH, Münster (page 37 below), Jos. Jeiter, Hadamar (page 34), Josse-Lalance & Cie, Paris (page 36 below), Joseph Klima Jr., Detroit (page 82), Raymond Laniepce, Paris (pages 88, 128, 186), Louis Loose, Brussels (page 79), Meusy, Besançon (page 176), Ministry of Public Building & Works, London (page 48 below), Paolo Monti, Milan (page 49 below), Werner Neumeister, Munich (page 35 below), Karl H. Paulmann, Berlin (page 35 right), La Photothèque, Paris (pages 71 and 94), Jochen Remmer, Lübeck (page 28), Roger-Viollet, Paris (page 47 above), Umberto Rossi, Venice (pages 60, 91), Oscar Savio, Rome (pages 27, 63, 80, 185), Tom Scott, Edinburgh (page 192), Walter Steinkopf, Berlin (page 98), Zoltan Wegner, London (pages 99, 140, 162, 167, 168, 184, 191), World-Press-Foto, Frankfurt-am-Main (page 37 above), and by courtesy of the photographic services of the following museums and galleries: Amsterdam, Rijksmuseum (page 124 above), Baltimore, Walters Art Gallery (page 152 upper right), Berlin, Staatliche Museen (pages 69, 70, 211), Cambridge, Mass., Fogg Art Museum (page 122 above), Florence, Soprintendenza alle Gallerie (page 175 lower left), Greenwich, National Maritime Museum (page 169), London, British Museum (page 177 and 200 above), London, National Gallery (page 108 upper left), Munich, Theater-Museum (page 110 below), Munich, Staatliche Graphische Sammlung (page 108 upper right), New York, Metropolitan Museum of Art (pages 174 lower left, 200), New York, Pierpont Morgan Library (page 36 upper right), Oxford, Ashmolean Museum (page 123), Paris, Bibliothèque Nationale (pages 46 above, 111, 153 above, 202 and 203), Salzburg, Mozarteum (page 142), Stockholm, Nationalmuseum (pages 81 and 131), Vienna, Österreichische Galerie (page 155 upper right), Windsor Castle, Library (pages 174 and 175 above), Zurich, Kunsthaus (page 154 below).

PRINTED IN SWITZERLAND